by Carolyn T. Kelley

Illustrated by Marcia Berntson Sims

International Marine Publishing Company

Camden, Maine

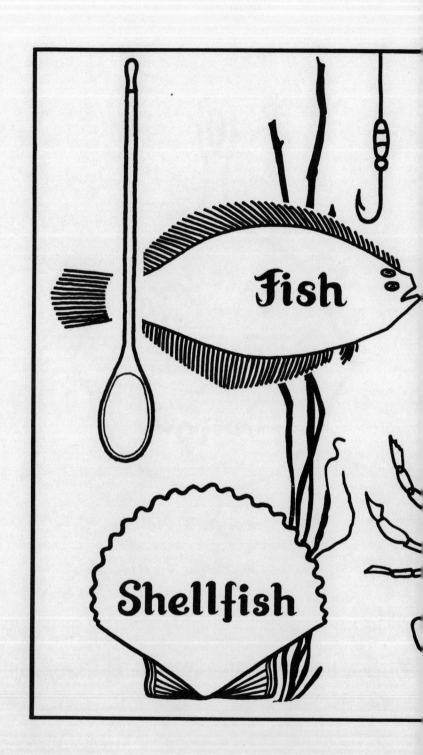

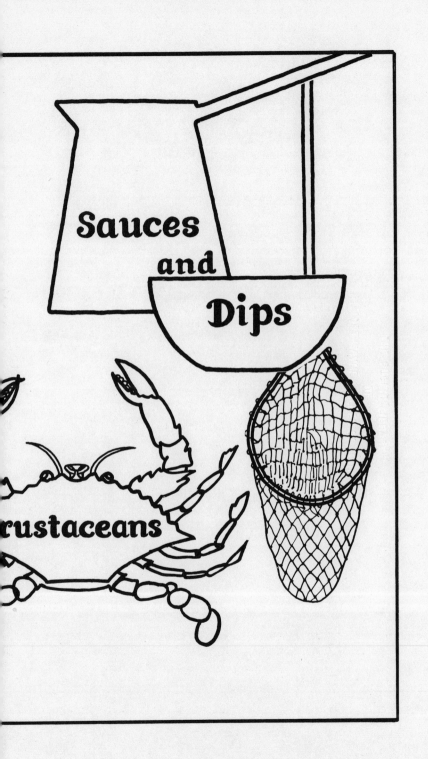

Sauces
and
Dips

Crustaceans

1761446

CONTENTS

PREFACE

The world is so full of a number of things.
I'm sure we should all be as happy as kings.

Robert Louis Stevenson

To those who wish to share my happiness, which is
cooking: I hope this book will provide many hours of
delightful entertainment, savory contentment, and fun-
filled hours of culinary experimenting. Please enjoy this
collection of recipes that have appeared in the *National
Fisherman* each month for almost the last ten years.

The "cookery" art found in this recipe book is a
myriad of satisfying dishes, as in this case, prepared with
fish and shellfish. From the shores of Maryland we have
presented the delicious concoctions including Maryland
crab. What tastes finer than hot, peppery, fried Maryland crabs? Cooks from all eras have played a part in
offering their tastiest recipes.

Boston scrod is enjoyed by New Englanders who have
passed their recipes along with the delicious stuffed
quahogs so frequently found all over the Cape Cod area.
Stuffed, baked bass, tasty to the last mouthful, is a must
in most New England homes, and we have found intrigu-
ing recipes from other parts of the country, too.

Other recipes playing a great part in most "Down East"
homes are clam chowders, scallop stew, and a variety of
fish chowders. After a big deep-sea fishing trip, what's
more fun than to make a huge, hot, chowder made out
of the haddock or other fish you have caught?

Acadian recipes handed from family to family feature salmon, togue, and other saltwater fish. Salmon steaks served with a slice of lemon are so simple, yet so tasty. Big thick slices of togue resemble Atlantic salmon so much that you hardly know what you're eating. The pink juicy steaks are a delightful gourmet's feast. Recipes for sauces, chowders, and planked fish passed on to us from all parts of Canada feature extra touches — such as French wines and delightful herbs added to them to make just the right flavor.

Shrimp recipes from Louisiana, Texas, and all over the South provide an interesting menu for all. Baked, stuffed shrimp is a favorite with everyone.

Clam bakes and boiled lobsters are featured attractions for summer picnics. Baked, stuffed lobsters are a delight to everyone. Recipes for fish dips, salmon balls, and all these fine foods are to be found in this recipe book, so enjoy your cooking.

I wish to thank everybody who has shared in making my food columns, and this book, a success. Among those who have contributed much information, recipes, and pictures are the United States Department of Fish and Wildlife, and the Department of Fisheries and Forestry of Canada.

Carolyn T. Kelley
Camden, Maine

FOREWORD

Carolyn Kelley's "Getting The Best From Seafood" column has been a fixture in the pages of *National Fisherman* for nearly ten years and, judging from the response, a popular one. With access to recipes from test kitchens in both the United States and Canada, with contributions from readers all over the world, and with scores of good-eating ideas from her own extensive collection of recipes, she has given her followers an unusual opportunity to get the very best of eating out of the versatile resource which is seafood.

If there has been one steady "complaint" from her following, it has concerned the lack of a compact collection of her recipes, a lack which ends with this book. Here, in easy-to-read, easy-to-use and especially, easy-to-eat form are some of her favorite ways to prepare and serve seafood. We're sure that this book will provide readers with some delicious new discoveries in their exploration of seafood cookery, a field as challenging and endless as the seas themselves.

David R. Getchell
Editor, *National Fisherman*

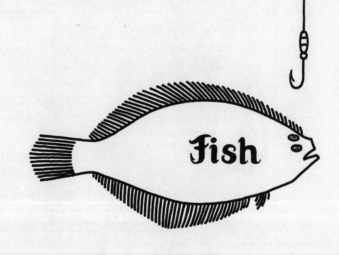

CLEANING FISH

Fish can be scaled, skinned, filleted, or cut into steaks. Naturally, the method you use will depend on the type of fish on hand as well as how it will be cooked.

To scale a fish, scrape the scales off with a knife or a special fish scaler, then wash the fish thoroughly. Cut open the belly, remove the entrails, and cut off the head, tail, and fins. Some fish that are scaled are striped bass, scup, and bluefish.

To skin a fish, cut along the top of the backbone from the head to the tail. Begin working with the back of the fish where the skin is darkest. Loosen the skin and draw it off gradually so as not to tear the flesh. After all of the skin has been removed, cut off the head and tail, and remove the entrails. Such fish as eels, cod, flounder, and catfish are commonly skinned.

Fish that have been skinned or scaled can also be filleted, a process that removes the bones. Carefully cut the flesh away on either side of the backbone, loosen the rib bones, and remove the entire skeleton intact. Some fish that are commonly filleted are flounder, cod, and haddock. For that matter, all fish can be filleted.

Skinned or scaled fish can also be cut into steaks. Remove the entrails, and cut off the head and tail. Cut across the fish at a 90-degree angle to the backbone. Slice the steaks off at the desired thickness. Such fish as swordfish, tuna, and salmon can be cut into steaks.

SAUCES TO SERVE WITH FISH

FRIED, BAKED, BROILED FISH

Tartar
Lemon butter
Catsup
Chili
Hollandaise
Mushroom
Bearnaise
Tomato

BOILED FISH

White sauce with any of the following ingredients:

Egg
Cheese
Shrimp
Olives
Pimento
Parsley

RELISHES TO SERVE WITH FISH

Coleslaw
Pickled beets
Cranberry sauce
Tart jellies
Applesauce

GARNISHES TO SERVE WITH FISH

Lemon wedges
Minced parsley
Fried apple rings
Spiced apples
Glazed pineapple

FISH BARBECUED IN FOIL

Fish is tasty when baked in foil. Cooking time depends on the size of the fish, but fillets only require about twenty minutes. Season your fish to taste with salt and pepper, and add a dash of lemon juice. Roll the fish in corn meal. Place a small piece of butter on the foil before you lay the fish on it. Wrap the fish tightly and fold the ends of the foil up. Place the fish on a grate over hot coals. The fish can be served in or out of the foil.

BARBECUED FISHBURGERS

Here's a succulent sandwich that's a treat for all:
Use 1 to 2 pounds of fish fillets. Brush them with butter; salt and pepper to taste. Broil them over coals until the fish loses its transparency and flakes easily — about 10 minutes. Serve the fish in hamburger buns with sandwich spread (tartar sauce) to taste.

FISH CHOWDER

2 pounds haddock or other fish
¼ pound of pork (sliced thin)
1 large onion, diced
3 large potatoes, diced
2 tablespoons parsley
1½ quarts of milk
1 bay leaf
1/8 teaspoon pepper
1 teaspoon salt

Fry the salt pork for about 15 minutes until it is golden brown and then put it to one side. Boil the fish in a pan with very little water — about 2 cups will be fine — for about 10 minutes until the fish flakes easily. Drain off the water and use it as stock to cook the potatoes and onion in. Remove the bones from the fish. After the potatoes are tender, add the salt pork and fish. Pour in the milk with the seasonings, and let the chowder come to the boiling point. Take it off the heat and allow it to set for 10 minutes before serving.

FISH BARBECUE

Barbecues and cookouts are favorite ways to serve an appetizing meal in the summer. For some reason, food cooked outside tastes so much better — your appetite is larger and fresh air makes the smell of open-fire cooking really tantalizing.

During your cookouts try this delicious meal, all prepared over coals:

BARBECUE SAUCE

1½ tablespoons Wesson Oil
½ cup minced onion
1¼ cups chili sauce
1/3 cup steak sauce
1 teaspoon horseradish

BARBECUED FISH

Use inch-thick fillets (1 to 2 pounds). Thaw if frozen. Brush the fillets with barbecue sauce. Place in a greased, folding-wire broiler and cook over hot coals until the fish loses its transparency and flakes easily.

BAKED POTATOES

Cook your potatoes in the following manner: Scrub medium baking potatoes. Dry and then rub them with cooking oil. Pierce each potato with your knife for quicker cooking. Wrap each potato in heavy aluminum foil. Place them on hot coals and cook about ¾ hour. Turn them once in a while to insure even cooking. When they are done, open the foil and cut the potatoes. Squeeze them open and add butter.

CALIFORNIA COLE SLAW

The salad to complete this meal is this delicious cole slaw:

1 envelope Lipton onion soup mix
1 pint dairy sour cream
2 quarts shredded cabbage
4 medium carrots, grated
1 medium green pepper, chopped
4 teaspoons cider vinegar

Blend the onion soup mix with the sour cream, and add the cabbage, carrots, green pepper, and vinegar; mix well. Cover and chill.

Plan to have fruit for dessert, and your meal is quick, easy, and fun!

FAST FISH CHOWDER

1 pound fish fillets
2 (10 ounce) cans frozen condensed cream of potato soup
2 soup cans milk
2 tablespoons chopped green
   onions and tops

If the fillets are frozen, thaw them slightly. Cut the fish into 1" by 2" pieces. Combine the soup and milk, and bring it to simmering temperature. Add the fish and onions, and reheat to simmering temperature. Cook the chowder below the boiling point for 5 to 10 minutes, or until the fish flakes easily when tested with a fork. Serve very hot. If desired, each serving can be garnished with a pat of butter. This recipe makes 7 cups. It was tested by the Department of Fisheries of Canada.

KEDGEREE

1 cup rice, steamed
4 hard-cooked eggs
3 tablespoons chopped parsley
2 cups cooked or canned fish,
    flaked with fork
½ cup cream
Salt and pepper, and curry if
    desired

This is a tasty casserole that can be varied with curry and that is a good way to serve some of the more bland fishes, such as hake or pollock. Kedgeree is also a good way to make a second, entirely different dish with the leftover fish from a bake. Merely mix all the ingredients together and warm it to just below the boiling point.

PICKLED FISH

1 pound fish
2 tablespoons oil
½ cup water
½ cup vinegar
2 tablespoons minced onion
1 tablespoon mixed pickling
    spice or 1 bay leaf
½ green or red pepper, diced
1 teaspoon salt
1/8 teaspoon pepper

Gently simmer the fish in salted water until it is cooked, or use leftover fried fish. Mix the remaining ingredients together in a bowl. Add the fish and gently turn it in this mixture. Cover the fish and let it stand in the refrigerator for at least 24 hours before serving. Turn the fish occasionally. Serve it cold, as a relish, or as a main dish. Makes 2½ cups. This pickled fish will keep for 2 weeks in the refrigerator.

DEVILED SCROD

1½ to 2 pounds of scrod (small
    haddock or cod)
¼ cup chopped green pepper
1 large onion, minced
1 tablespoon prepared mustard
1 teaspoon Worcestershire sauce
1/8 teaspoon Tabasco
3½ tablespoons lemon juice
½ cup butter or margarine
2 cups fine, soft bread crumbs
2 tablespoons grated Parmesan
    cheese

Wipe the scrod with a damp cloth and cut it into 4 portions. Combine the green pepper, onion, mustard, Worcestershire sauce, Tabasco, and lemon juice. Melt the butter and stir in the bread crumbs; add this to the vegetable mixture. Season the scrod with salt and pepper, and dot with butter. Place it on a foil-lined broiler rack about 4 inches below the heat, and broil for 5 minutes. Turn the scrod and top it with the bread mixture. Return it to the broiler for 5 to 7 minutes, or until the fish flakes easily. Sprinkle the top with Parmesan cheese and then broil the scrod for 1 more minute.

FISH-STICK PASTRIES

Pie crust or pastry mix
Prepared mustard
Sharp cheese
One box fish sticks

Roll the pastry and cut it into 3-inch squares. Spread a little mustard on each square and then lay across a strip of cheese, followed by a fish stick. Fold over opposite corners and hold the pastry together with a toothpick. Put the pastries on a cookie sheet and bake in a very hot oven (450° F) for about 15 minutes.

BISCUIT FISH ROLL

2 cups sifted all-purpose flour
3 teaspoons baking powder
1 teaspoon salt
4 tablespoons shortening
2/3 cup milk, approximately

Mix and sift the flour, baking powder, and salt. Cut in the shortening until the mixture resembles fine bread crumbs. Add the milk slowly to make a soft, but not sticky dough. Toss the dough on a floured board and roll it lightly until it is ½" thick. Spread the fish filling over the dough, and roll it up as if it were a jelly roll. Pinch the edge, and prick the top with a fork in several places. Put the roll on a baking sheet and bake it in a very hot oven (425° F) for approximately 20 minutes, or until it is golden brown.

This recipe can be varied by replacing 2 tablespoons of the milk with 1 beaten egg.

FISH FILLING

2 cups cooked flaked fish
1 teaspoon salt
1 tablespoon minced onion
1 tablespoon lemon juice

Mix together the cooked fish, salt, minced onion, and lemon juice. Spread the filling over the biscuit dough. This should yield 6 servings.

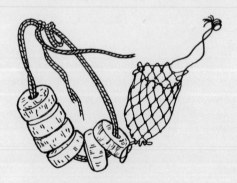

10

FISH CAKES

1 cup cooked fish
1½ cups mashed potatoes
1 egg, beaten
1 tablespoon melted butter
Salt and pepper to taste
½ teaspoon onion juice
Fine bread crumbs

Use any cooked fish you happen to have around the house. Flake a cup full. Mix the first six ingredients together and form into cakes ½" thick and 3" in diameter. Cover them with fine bread crumbs. Sauté the cakes in bacon, salt-pork fat or butter until they're nice and brown. Serves 3 to 4.

FISH BAKED IN WHITE WINE

4 fillets
½ cup consommé
Juice of 1 lemon
¼ cup cream
2 egg yolks, beaten
½ cup dry sauterne wine
2 ounces butter
8 mushrooms (or 1 small can sautéed)
Salt and pepper

Saute the mushrooms and keep them hot. Place the fillets in a baking dish. Blend the wine and consommé with the lemon juice and pour it over the fish. Add salt and pepper to taste. Bake the fish for 20 minutes. Pour off the juice the fish was baked in and add it to the beaten egg yolks mixed with the cream. Thicken the sauce by adding a little flour and putting it over a flame. Pour the sauce over the fish. Garnish the fish with onions and, if desired, place it under the broiler for 1 minute before serving.

FISH DISH

1 cup spaghetti, cooked
1 can tuna fish
1/3 cup pimento, diced
½ cup nut meats (cashews or
    walnuts)
1 can mushroom soup
¾ cup milk
1 cup grated cheese

Mix the above ingredients and put the mixture in a greased baking dish. Bake for 40 minutes in a 350° F oven.

CHINESE FISH AND GREENS

1 pound fish fillets
1 pound fresh broccoli
3 tablespoons salad oil
1 teaspoon salt
1 teaspoon cornstarch
½ cup water

Thaw the fillets, if they are frozen. Cut the fish into pieces about 2" by 1". Slice the broccoli lengthwise into thin pieces. Rinse it with cold water. Heat 2 table-spoons of oil in a frying pan. Drop the wet broccoli carefully into the hot fat and sprinkle it with ½ teaspoon of salt. Cook the broccoli, stirring constantly, over high heat for 5 minutes or until it is tender but still crisp and green. Remove the broccoli and keep it hot. Heat the remaining tablespoon of oil in a pan. Sprinkle the fish with the remaining ½ teaspoon of salt. Cook it in hot fat for 1 to 2 minutes on each side. When the fish is opaque and flakes easily when tested with a fork, remove it and keep it hot with the broccoli. Combine the corn-starch and water. Add this mixture to any juices remain-ing in the pan. Cook and stir the sauce until it is clear and thickened. Pour it over the fish and broccoli. This recipe makes 4 servings, with about 190 calories per serving.

FISH AND CHEESE CASSEROLE

1 pound frozen fish fillets —
    haddock, flounder, or halibut
½ cup milk
½ pound finely cut sharp cheddar
    cheese
¼ teaspoon paprika
¼ teaspoon parsley
¼ teaspoon dry mustard
¼ teaspoon Worcestershire sauce
2 cups soft bread crumbs — use
    blender if possible

Cut the fish into pieces and put it in a casserole. Combine the milk, cheese, and seasonings in the top of a double boiler. Cook this over boiling water, stirring constantly, until the cheese melts. Add the bread crumbs and pour the sauce over the fish. Bake the casserole at 375° F until it is puffy and lightly browned on top (about 25 minutes).

SAUCY FISH FILLETS

1 pound whitefish fillets
    (other fillets may be substituted)
1 can (10½ ounces) condensed
    cream of mushroom soup

If you are using frozen fish, thaw it and blot dry first. Arrange the fish in a shallow baking dish (10"x6"x2"). Stir the soup in the can, and then pour it over the fish. Use your favorite topping or the one that follows. Bake at 400° F for 20 minutes. This will make 4 servings. To vary the recipe, use cream of celery soup in place of the cream of mushroom.

TOPPING

Combine ½ cup of shredded cheddar cheese, chopped parsley, paprika, and corn flakes or toast cubes. Garnish with thin lemon slices.

13

FESTIVAL FILLETS

2 pounds fish fillets, fresh
   or frozen
½ teaspoon salt
1/8 teaspoon pepper
3 cups soft bread cubes
6 tablespoons butter or other
   fat
1 cup chopped onion
1 teaspoon powdered mustard
1 cup grated cheddar cheese
¼ cup chopped parsley

Thaw the fillets, if frozen, and cut them into 6 equal portions. Season them with salt and pepper, and place them in a single layer in a shallow greased baking pan or dish. Toast the crumbs lightly in a slow oven. Melt the butter and add the onion, and then sauté until it is tender but not browned; stir in the mustard. Combine the toasted crumbs and the onion mixture. Add the cheese and parsley, and mix thoroughly. Spread this sauce over the fillet portions. Bake the fish in a moderate oven (350° F) for 20 to 25 minutes, or until the fish flakes easily when tested with a fork. This recipe makes 6 servings.

FISH CASSEROLE

1 can frozen cream of shrimp soup
½ pound raw haddock, cut small
½ pound scallops, cut small
¼ cup cracker crumbs
Paprika

Combine the soup, haddock, and scallops and put them in a buttered casserole. Top the mixture with crumbs and paprika and dot it with butter. Bake for ¾ hour at 350° F.

FISH A LA CREOLE

1½ cups flaked fish — halibut,
    cod, or other
2 tablespoons butter
2 tablespoons flour
1 cup tomato juice
2 tablespoons chopped onion
2 tablespoons green pepper
¼ cup dried bread crumbs

Melt the butter and stir in the flour. Mix in the tomato juice and cook until the sauce has thickened a little. Add the other ingredients and put the mixture into a greased casserole. Top it with the bread crumbs, add slices of butter, and brown in the oven at 400° F.

TASTY FISH LOAF

3 cups corn flakes, crushed
1½ cups milk
2 cups cooked fish, flaked
1/3 cup sour cream
¼ cup minced onion
1 tablespoon chopped parsley
1 tablespoon lemon juice
½ teaspoon Worcestershire
    sauce
¼ teaspoon thyme
1 teaspoon salt
Dash of pepper
2 eggs, well beaten

Fresh or frozen fish of any type, as well as canned tuna or salmon, will work well in this recipe.
Combine the corn flakes and milk, and allow it to set for about 10 minutes. Add the remaining ingredients, except for the eggs; beat thoroughly. Fold in the beaten eggs, and beat again. Turn this into a well-greased quart loaf pan and bake in a moderate oven (370° F) for 50 to 60 minutes. Serve this fish loaf with white sauce seasoned with 1 teaspoon mustard.

BROILED FILLETS WITH MUSHROOMS

2 pounds fillets
¼ cup melted butter or oil
1 teaspoon salt
Dash of pepper
2 cans mushroom stems and
    pieces, drained
1 cup grated cheddar cheese
2 tablespoons chopped
    parsley

Thaw the fillets, if frozen, and cut them into suitable pieces for serving. Combine the butter, salt, and pepper, and mix thoroughly. Chop up the mushrooms and mix them with the cheese and parsley. Place the fish on a well-greased broiler pan and brush with fat. Broil the fish for about 3 minutes about 3 inches from the source of heat. Turn the fish carefully and brush with the remaining fat. Broil it 3 to 4 minutes more, or until the fish flakes easily when tested with a fork. Spread the mushroom mixture on the fish and broil it 2 to 3 minutes more, or until it is lightly browned.

BROILED FISH

2 pounds fish fillets or steaks
    (fresh or frozen)
1 teaspoon salt
1/8 teaspoon pepper
4 tablespoons butter or other
    fat, melted

Cut the fish into serving-size portions and sprinkle both sides with salt and pepper. Place the fish on a preheated greased broiler pan about 2 inches from the heat. If the skin has not been removed from the fillets, put the skin side up. Brush the fish with melted fat or butter. Broil it for 5 to 8 minutes, or until it flakes easily. Garnish and serve.

DEEP-FRIED FISH

2 pounds haddock fillets, or other
  fish
1 egg, beaten
1 tablespoon milk
1 teaspoon salt
Dash pepper
½ cup flour
1 cup cracker crumbs, rolled ex-
  ceptionally fine

Cut the fish into bite-size pieces. Combine the egg, milk, and seasonings. Dip the fish into the egg mixture and roll it in flour and crumbs. Fry the fish in deep fat at 375° F for 2 to 4 minutes, or until it is golden brown. Drain the fish on paper towels. Serve it with tartar sauce.

FRIED FISH

2 pounds of dressed fish
  (whole fillets or steaks)
1 egg
2 tablespoons water
1 cup prepared biscuit mix
3 tablespoons ketchup
½ cup shortening or oil

First dip the fish in the egg beaten with water, then dip it in the biscuit mix blended with ketchup. Fry the fish slowly in heated shortening until it is golden brown on both sides. Serve it with lemon and parsley.

FISH FRIED IN GARLIC BUTTER

3 eggs, beaten
4 tablespoons milk
½ teaspoon garlic salt
Flour (about ½ cup)
Fresh or frozen fish, thawed

Combine the eggs, milk, garlic salt, salt, and pepper. Add enough flour to make a thin batter. Dip the fish in batter and fry over medium heat until the fish browns and flakes easily.

FISH PUFF

1 cup cooked fish
1 cup mashed potatoes
½ cup milk
2 eggs
Salt and pepper

Mix together the cooked fish, mashed potatoes, milk, salt, and pepper. Stir in 1 well-beaten egg. Turn this into an earthenware casserole and heat in the oven at 350° F. Beat the white of another egg and fold into it the beaten yolk seasoned with salt and pepper. Heap this mixture over the fish and brown it in the oven. This recipe serves 6.

BAKED SURPRISE

2 large fillets or steaks (3 pounds)
1 quart milk
4 medium-sized onions
1 quart of sliced white potatoes
Salt and pepper

Put the fish in a baking pan. If you are using fillets, put the skin side down. Arrange the potatoes and onions around the fish, and pour seasoned milk over this. Cook slowly in a moderate oven (350° F) until thoroughly done.

PARTY FISH BALL

2 cups canned salmon (remove
   the bones)
1 8-ounce package cream cheese,
   softened
1 tablespoon lemon juice
2 teaspoons horseradish
½ teaspoon basil
1 teaspoon liquid smoke
½ cup chopped pecans or walnuts
2 tablespoons chopped parsley

*Drain the fish and debone it. Mix thoroughly the
cheese, lemon juice, basil, horseradish, liquid smoke,
and salmon. Chill thoroughly for several hours. Shape
the mixture into a ball and roll in the nuts mixed with
parsley.*

BROILED FILLETS WITH
TOMATO AND CHEESE

1 pound cod or other fish fillets,
   fresh or frozen
½ teaspoon salt
2 tablespoons minced onion
4 tomato slices
2 tablespoons melted butter or
   margarine
½ cup grated cheddar cheese

*Thaw the frozen fillets; cut the fish into 4 serving-size
portions. Place the fish in a shallow, greased baking pan.
Season it with salt and spread with minced onion. Top
each portion with a tomato slice. Spoon the fish with
melted butter. Broil the fish 6" to 8" from the source
of heat for about 15 minutes, or until the fish flakes
easily when tested with a fork. Remove from the oven
and sprinkle with grated cheese. Continue broiling just
long enough to melt the cheese. Makes 4 servings.*

BAKED FISH WITH CHEESE SAUCE

2 tablespoons butter
2 tablespoons flour
1 teaspoon dry mustard
1 cup milk
½ teaspoon salt
1/8 teaspoon pepper

Make a sauce of these ingredients in the top of a double boiler and add 1 cup of grated cheese (American or other). Stir until the sauce is blended. Pour it over 1 pound of uncooked haddock fillets in a buttered baking dish. Bake the fish for 25 to 30 minutes in a 350°F oven.

FLOUNDER ROLL-UPS

12 large flounder fillets, fresh or
    frozen
8 strips bacon, diced
½ cup melted butter or margarine
6 cups cornbread crumbs
½ teaspoon dried chervil
½ teaspoon dried tarragon leaves
Hot water
Butter or margarine

If you are using frozen fillets, defrost them. Cook the bacon until it is crisp and drain it on absorbent paper. Drain off the bacon drippings from the pan and use ¼ cup of it to mix with the melted butter. To this, add the bread crumbs, bacon, and herbs and mix well. Add enough hot water to make the stuffing as moist as you wish. Put a spoonful of stuffing on each fillet and roll it up tightly. Line a baking pan with foil, and grease the foil. Put the roll-ups in the pan and dot them generously with butter or margarine. Bake them at 375°F for 25 minutes, or until the fish flakes easily with a fork. Serve the roll-ups with a sauce of your choice. This recipe makes 6 to 8 servings.

CODFISH DELMONICO

1 small cod (scrod)
Butter
Salt
Pepper
Juice of 1 lemon
1 tablespoon of chopped parsley
1 chopped onion
Fine bread crumbs

Split and bone the small cod. Put it in a buttered baking pan with the skin down. Coat the fish with melted butter and the juice of 1 lemon, and sprinkle it with salt, pepper, 1 tablespoon of chopped parsley, 1 chopped onion, and fine bread crumbs. Bake it in a pre-heated oven at 350° F until the crumbs are brown. Cooking time should be about 25 minutes. Serve the fish, garnished with lemon, on a platter.

CELERY FLOUNDER ROLLUPS

1 can (10½ ounces) condensed
   cream of celery soup
1 cup cooked rice
1/3 cup chopped pecans
1/8 teaspoon tarragon, crushed
6 flounder fillets, about 1½
   pounds
¼ cup sour cream
2 tablespoons chopped parsley
Paprika
Lemon wedges

Combine ¼ cup of soup with the rice, nuts, and tarragon. Put about 2 tablespoons of this rice mixture on each fillet. Roll up the fillets, fasten them with toothpicks, and place them in a skillet. Blend the remaining soup with the sour cream and parsley, and pour the mixture over the fillets. Cover the skillet and cook the fish for 20 minutes over low heat. Sprinkle the fish with paprika and garnish with lemon wedges. Makes 6 servings.

COD WITH EGG SAUCE

2 pounds frozen cod fillets
1½ cups milk
½ teaspoon salt
¼ cup butter or margarine
¼ cup flour
½ teaspoon dry mustard
¼ teaspoon salt
1/8 teaspoon white pepper
2 hard-cooked eggs, chopped
2 tablespoons finely chopped
    parsley

Thaw the fillets slightly and cut them into serving-size portions. Put the pieces in one layer in a shallow, greased baking dish. Combine the milk and ½ teaspoon of salt, and pour it over the fish. Bake the fish in a moderate oven (350° F) for 30 minutes, or until the fish has lost its watery look. The fish should be milky white throughout and should flake easily when tested with a fork. Remove the fish from the oven and pour off the milk, which will be used to make the sauce. Keep the fish warm.

To make the sauce, melt the butter and then blend in the flour, mustard, ¼ teaspoon salt, and pepper. Cook the sauce over low heat until it is bubbly; stir constantly. Add the hot milk, and then cook and stir some more until it is smoothly thickened. Add the eggs and parsley. Pour the sauce over the fish and reheat for several minutes, or, carefully remove the fish to a heated platter and garnish to taste. Serve the sauce separately at the table. This makes 6 servings.

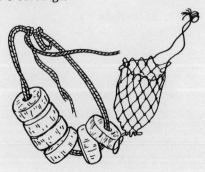

NEW ENGLAND
SALT CODFISH DINNER

1½ to 2 pounds salt cod
¼ pound salt pork
6 potatoes
12 small beets
6 onions
1½ cups hot white sauce
2 hard-cooked eggs, diced

*Cut the fish into serving portions. Freshen it for 2 to
3 hours in cold water, and then bring the water to a boil.
Drain the water from the fish. Dice the salt pork and fry
it until brown. Cook the vegetables separately until they
are tender. Arrange the fish on a hot platter and cover
with the white sauce, which has been mixed with the
diced, hard-cooked eggs. Garnish the fish with the crisp
salt pork and arrange the vegetables around the edge of
the platter. This serves 6.*

SALT COD AND POTATOES

1 pound of salt cod
5 medium-sized potatoes
½ pound salt pork
1 onion

*Tear the salt cod into small pieces and put it in cold
water. Bring it to a boil, drain off the water, and again
immerse the cod in cold water. Do this three times, but
the last time let the salt cod cook 20 minutes. Slice the
potatoes about ½ inch thick and add them to the salt cod.
Cook until the potatoes are tender, then drain and put
the fish and potatoes on a platter. While cooking the
potatoes, slice the pork in thin strips and fry it. Slice an
onion into the pork and allow it to brown nicely. Pour
the pork and onions over the hot potatoes and fish. Serve
at once. Some people prefer to serve this meal with cooked beets, either buttered or pickled.*

SALT FISH WITH EGGS

2 cups salt fish
4 hard-cooked eggs
2 cups white sauce

Soak the fish overnight, then drain and cover with fresh water. Simmer the fish for about 15 minutes. Add the fish to the white sauce and stir for a minute, then add 2 sliced eggs. Pour this over quartered, hot, boiled potatoes, which have been arranged on a platter. Slice the last 2 eggs and use them for garnish.

HALIBUT-LOBSTER CASSEROLE

3 cups cooked rice
2 cups flaked boiled halibut
1 cup lobster meat
1 can pimento, sliced
2 cups milk
1 cup cream
¼ cup butter
5 tablespoons chopped onion
1 tablespoon chopped green
   pepper
¼ cup shredded cheese
2 tablespoons sherry
Salt and pepper to taste

Melt the butter, blend in the flour, then add the milk and cream. Cook this, stirring constantly until it has thickened. Sauté the onion and green pepper in a little butter, and add this to the sauce. Mix the remaining ingredients into the sauce. Put the casserole into a buttered baking dish and cover it with buttered crumbs. Bake it for 30 minutes at 350° F. This serves 8 to 10 people. The feature of this dish is that the halibut captures the flavor of the lobster.

BAKED HALIBUT

**2 pounds halibut fillets
Sliced onions
Butter
Juice of ½ lemon
½ cup white wine
Cucumbers**

*Place a few thin slices of onion in a baking dish —
enough to cover the bottom of a dish to contain 2
pounds of halibut fillets. Place the fillets on top of the
sliced onions. Dot with butter, season with lemon juice,
and pour ½ cup of white wine around the fish. Cook
the fish for ½ hour, basting often. Serve it with hollandaise sauce and cucumbers.*

HOLLANDAISE SAUCE

**½ cup butter
½ cup boiling water
4 teaspoons lemon juice
2 egg yolks
¼ teaspoon salt
Pinch of cayenne**

*Break the egg yolks into the top section of a double
boiler; beat them lightly; add lemon juice; beat them
again. In a separate bowl, cream the butter and add it
to the egg mixture; blend them well. Insert the top section of the double boiler into the lower section, which
has been half filled with boiling water. Place it over the
flame; cook the sauce until the butter melts and the mixture begins to thicken, stirring constantly. Add the salt
and cayenne; stir gently; add boiling water very slowly
and continue stirring until the sauce is smooth. Serve
immediately.*

BATTER-FRIED HALIBUT

2 pounds halibut steaks or other
    fresh fish sticks
1 teaspoon salt
1 cup sifted flour
1 teaspoon baking powder
¾ cup milk
1 teaspoon marjoram (if desired)
½ teaspoon salt
¼ teaspoon pepper
1 egg, beaten

Thaw the steaks, if frozen. Remove the skin and bones from the steaks, and cut them into 1½ inch cubes. Sprinkle them with salt. Sift together the flour, baking powder, marjoram, salt, and pepper. Combine the milk and the egg, and blend into the flour mixture. Dip the fish cubes in the batter and fry them in a basket in deep fat, 375° F, for 2 minutes or until they are golden brown. Drain the fish on absorbent paper. This serves 6.

HADDOCK PARMESAN

2 pounds haddock fillets or other
    frozen fish
1 cup sour cream
¼ cup grated parmesan cheese
1 tablespoon lemon juice
1 tablespoon grated onion
¼ teaspoon salt
Dash tabasco
Paprika

Thaw the fillets, skin them, and cut them into serving-size portions. Place them in a single layer in a well-greased baking dish, 12"x18"x2". Combine the remaining ingredients, except the paprika, and spread the mixture over the fish. Sprinkle the fish with paprika. Bake the fish in a moderate oven, 350° F, for 25 to 30 minutes, or until the fish flakes easily when tested with a fork. Serves 6.

HADDOCK MASQUERADE

2 pounds haddock fillets or other
　　fish fillets
½ teaspoon salt
Dash pepper
1 egg, beaten
3 tablespoons grated parmesan
　　cheese
½ cup dry bread crumbs
1 can (10½ ounces) marinara
　　spaghetti sauce
½ pound mozzarella cheese,
　　sliced thin
1 tablespoon grated cheese
　　(parmesan)

*Thaw the frozen fillets, skin them, and cut them into
serving-size portions. Add the seasonings to the egg and
mix well. Combine 3 tablespoons of grated parmesan
cheese and the crumbs. Dip the fish in the egg and roll
it in crumbs. Fry it in hot fat at moderate heat until it
is brown on one side. Turn the fish carefully and brown
it on the other side. Cooking time is approximately 6 to
8 minutes. Place the fish in a single layer in a well-greased baking dish, 12"x8"x2". Pour ¾ cup of the sauce
over the fish; top it with mozzarella cheese. Cover the
fish with the remaining sauce. Sprinkle the top with 1
tablespoon of parmesan cheese. Bake in a moderate
oven (350° F) for 30 to 40 minutes, or until the fish
flakes easily when tested with a fork. Serves 6.*

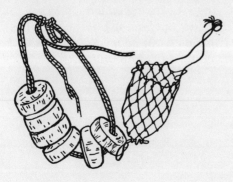

FINNAN HADDIE WITH SHRIMP

2 pounds finnan haddie, soaked
   in water 2 hours
1/8 pound butter
1 cup shrimp — fresh, canned,
   or frozen
1 small can mushroom pieces
2 hard-boiled eggs, sliced
2 tablespoons sherry
Cayenne pepper to taste
Cream sauce

*Melt the butter in a heavy skillet. Pull the soaked
fish apart in small pieces and put it in the skillet, which
should be kept hot, but not hot enough to burn the
butter. Sprinkle the fish with a little cayenne and stir
well for a few minutes. Add the cream sauce, shrimp,
mushrooms, and eggs, and simmer for 15 minutes. Add
the sherry and serve on toast.*

CREAM SAUCE

2 tablespoons butter
2 tablespoons flour
1 cup cream
¼ teaspoon salt
Few grains pepper

*Melt the butter in a saucepan, then add the flour mix-
ed with the seasonings. Stir well. Heat the cream and
pour it into the saucepan gradually, stirring constantly.
Bring the sauce to the boiling point and boil it for 2
minutes. This sauce can be made in a double boiler,
but must be cooked for 15 minutes.*

BAKED STUFFED HADDOCK FILLETS

2 haddock fillets
Salt and pepper
Lemon slices

Place a piece of aluminum foil, large enough to wrap your stuffed haddock fillets completely, in a baking tin. Place one fillet on the foil and fill it with mushroom stuffing. Place the other fillet on top and garnish it with the lemon slices. Wrap the fish up in the foil and bake it in the oven for 40 minutes at 375° F.

MUSHROOM STUFFING

Mix ½ cup of bread crumbs with 1 teaspoon parsley, 3 tablespoons melted butter, and ½ cup sliced mushrooms. Add ½ teaspoon salt and a dash of pepper.

BAKED FILLETS OF SOLE

1 large can of chopped mushroom
   pieces
4 or 5 cooked potatoes, sliced thin
2 tablespoons butter or margarine
1 teaspoon salt
1 teaspoon pepper
Paprika
2/3 cup white wine
1 cup commercial sour cream
2 pounds fresh fillets of sole
Parsley flakes

Place the potatoes in a buttered baking dish, about 12"x8". Add the mushrooms. Put pieces of butter on top, add half of the salt and pepper, and sprinkle with paprika. Pour the wine over everything, and then spread on half of the sour cream. Next, lay down the fish in pieces, and sprinkle over it the remaining salt, pepper, and a little paprika. Spread on the rest of the sour cream. Bake the fish for 45 minutes at 375° F. Garnish it with parsley.

BAKED CREAM HADDOCK FILLETS

2 pounds haddock fillets
¼ teaspoon salt
1/8 teaspoon pepper
1 can cream of celery soup
1 teaspoon prepared mustard
1 tablespoon minced parsley

Cut the fillets into serving pieces and place them in a greased, shallow pan. Sprinkle them with seasonings. Heat the celery soup and pour it over the fillets. Sprinkle the tops with buttered crumbs and parsley. Bake the fish for 35 minutes at 350° F. Serves 6.

FISH STUFFING

4 slices buttered bread
1 egg
¼ cup melted butter
2 medium onions
2 small pickles
Salt, pepper, poultry seasoning
   to taste
Milk to soften
1 tablespoon parsley flakes

This makes enough to stuff a 1½ to 2 pound fish.

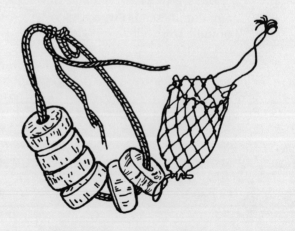

GLOUCESTER WHITING FLORENTINE
With Egg Noodles

1 package (8 ounces) medium
    egg noodles
3 tablespoons butter or margarine
3 tablespoons flour
3 cups milk
1 tablespoon lemon juice
1 teaspoon dry mustard
1 teaspoon Worcestershire sauce
½ teaspoon salt
1/8 teaspoon pepper
1/8 teaspoon nutmeg
1½ cups shredded sharp cheddar
    cheese
2 packages (10 ounce each) frozen
    chopped spinach, thawed and
    drained
1½ pounds whiting fillets
¼ cup toasted slivered blanched
    almonds (optional)

Cook the noodles as directed on the package until they are tender, then drain them. Meanwhile, melt the butter, blend in the flour, add the milk, and stir over medium heat until the sauce is smooth and thick. Stir in the lemon juice, Worcestershire sauce, salt, pepper, nutmeg, and 1 cup of cheese. Combine the cooked noodles with half of this cheese sauce, then pour it into a 2-quart baking dish and top it off with the spinach. Arrange the fish on the spinach and pour the remaining sauce over the fish. Sprinkle the top with the remaining cheese and the almonds. Bake at 375° F for 25 minutes, or until the fish is cooked.

31

CHOW MEIN LOAF

3 cups medium white sauce
2 egg yolks, well beaten
1 cup tuna (water packed)
½ cup toasted, split, blanched
    almonds
2 cups chow mein noodles
    (4 ounces)
2 egg whites, stiffly beaten

Using 1¼ cups of the white sauce, mix all the other ingredients together, with the exception of the egg whites, which should be folded in gently. Pour the mixture in a greased 9"x5"x3" pan. Bake at 350°F for 30 minutes. Unmold the loaf on a hot platter and serve it with the remaining sauce. If you wish, 2 tablespoons of capers or chopped pickles can be added to the sauce.

TUNA-STUFFED TOMATOES

2 cans (6 or 6½ ounce each) of
    tuna
6 large tomatoes
1 teaspoon salt
1 cup grated cheese
1 cup cooked rice
1 egg, beaten
Dash pepper
1 tablespoon melted fat or oil
¼ cup dry bread crumbs

Drain the tuna and break it into large pieces. Wash the tomatoes and remove the stem ends and centers; sprinkle with salt. Combine the cheese, rice, egg, pepper, and tuna, and stuff it in the tomatoes. Combine the fat and crumbs and sprinkle it over the top of the stuffed tomatoes. Place the tomatoes in a well-greased baking dish, 10"x6"x2". Bake them in a moderate oven (350°F) for 30 to 40 minutes, or until the tomatoes are tender. This recipe serves 6 people.

32

TUNAFISH CASSEROLE

1 can white chunk-style tunafish
   (or other variety if desired)
1 can mushroom soup
1 bag potato chips (3 cups crushed chips)
2 tablespoons milk

*Combine the tunafish, mushroom soup, and milk, and
mix them together thoroughly. Use a small aluminum
bread tin that has been greased with butter. Put one cup
of crushed potato chips in the bottom of the tin. Add a
layer of the tuna mixture (about half), then another cup
of crushed potato chips. Add one more layer of the tuna
mixture and sprinkle the rest of the potato chips on top.
With the oven at 350° F., brown the casserole slightly
and serve. This takes about 20 minutes to heat through
and brown. Incidentally, the potato chips do stay crisp.*

TUNA SKILLET SUPPER

½ cup chopped green pepper
½ cup sliced green onion
2 tablespoons butter or margarine
1 can (10½ ounces) condensed
   cream of celery soup
1/3 cup water
2 teaspoons vinegar
Generous dash pepper
2 tablespoons chopped pimento
3 cups sliced cooked potatoes
1 can (7 ounce) tuna, drained and
   flaked

*In a skillet, cook the green pepper and onion in butter
until they are tender. Stir in the soup, water, vinegar,
pepper, pimento, and potatoes. Add the tuna. Cover
and cook over low heat until it is hot. Stir now and then.
This makes 3 to 4 servings.*

TUNA-CASHEW CASSEROLE

1 cup tuna
1 cup creamed mushroom soup
1 cup celery, cut small
1 small package cashew nuts
Onions
¼ cup water
Chinese noodles

Divide the ingredients in half and put them in successive layers in a greased casserole in the following order: tuna, onions, soup, celery, and nuts. Put the other half of the ingredients on in layers in the same order. Top this with Chinese noodles and bake the casserole for ½ hour at 375° F.

CHOPSTICK TUNA

1 can (7 ounce) tuna
1 can (10 ounce) mandarin
    orange segments
1 can (10 ounce) condensed
    cream of mushroom soup
1 cup chopped celery
¼ cup chopped onion
½ cup salted, toasted cashews
1 can (3 ounce) chow-mein
    noodles

Drain the tuna and break it into bite-size chunks. Drain the mandarin orange segments, reserving ¼ cup of the juice. Combine the juice with the mushroom soup. Add the tuna, celery, onion, cashews, and half the noodles. Spoon the mixture into a greased, 5-cup casserole, sprinkle the remaining noodles over the top. Bake in a moderate oven (375° F) for about 20 minutes, or until well heated. Garnish with the mandarin orange segments. Makes 4 or 5 servings.

TUNABURGERS

1 can of white tuna, drained
(tuna packed in water pre-
ferred)
¾ can of mushroom soup,
not diluted
½ cup diced celery
½ cup sliced olives

*Mix the ingredients together. Add salt and pepper to
taste, and fill hamburger rolls with the mixture. Wrap
the hamburgers in foil and put them in the oven at 375°
F. Bake for about 25 minutes to ½ hour. Even when
prepared ahead, this mixture will not soak into the bread.*

TUNA-TOPPED PIZZA

1 cup biscuit mix   **1761446**
1/3 cup milk
1 (6½ ounce) can white chunk
tuna, drained
¼ cup sliced ripe olives
1 (8 ounce) can tomato sauce
with mushrooms
½ teaspoon oregano
¼ teaspoon garlic powder
1 cup shredded Mozzerella or
Swiss cheese

*Stir the biscuit mix and milk together to form dough.
Roll the dough ¼" thick on a floured surface. Place the
dough on an oiled baking sheet. Pinch the edge to form
a rim. Arrange the tuna and the olives on the dough;
pour the tomato sauce over the top. Sprinkle with oregano, garlic powder, and cheese. Bake at 425° F for 20
minutes.*

TUNA BUNS

1 can white tuna (packed in water)
1 chopped dill pickle
1 chopped onion
Mayonnaise

Mix the tuna, pickle, onion, and mayonnaise, and spread them on hamburger buns. Place the buns under the broiler for a few minutes.

TASTY SALMON LOAF

1 can salmon, flaked
1½ cups cracker crumbs
½ teaspoon salt
1 teaspoon parsley flakes
1 cup milk
2 eggs
2 tablespoons melted butter

Mix the ingredients together in the order given, and turn the mixture into a greased loaf pan. Cook the loaf at 350° F for 45 minutes.

SALMON SALAD

1 can red salmon
1 cup pitted ripe olives
2 cups diced cooked potatoes
½ cup sliced cucumber
1 small diced onion
½ cup sour cream
1 teaspoon salt
2 tablespoons cider vinegar
Pepper

Blend together the sour cream, salt, pepper, and vinegar. Add this to the salmon mixture. Serve the salad on crisp lettuce.

SALMON-POTATO PIE

1 can (15½ ounces) salmon
½ cup chopped onion
¼ cup butter, melted
6 medium potatoes, cooked
1/3 cup milk
½ teaspoon salt
1/8 teaspoon pepper
¼ teaspoon savory
Pastry for a one-crust pie

Empty the can of salmon, including the liquid, into a bowl. Mash the fish with a fork, combining it with the liquid. Sauté the onion in butter until it is limp but not browned. Mash the potatoes, then mix in the milk, the onions and butter, and the seasonings. Whip this until it is well blended and fluffy. Put half of the potato mixture in a greased 9" pie plate or a shallow, 1-quart baking dish and cover it with the salmon. Top the dish with the remaining potato and then cover it with the rolled out, pricked pastry. Brush the pastry lightly with milk. Bake the pie in a moderately hot oven (400° F) for about 30 minutes, or until the crust is golden brown. This recipe makes 6 servings.

SCALLOPED SALMON

1 pint of milk
2 eggs
1 chopped onion
2 tablespoons butter
3 tablespoons flour
Salt and pepper to taste
1 large can of salmon

Cook all of the above ingredients in a double boiler until they have thickened into a sauce. Remove the sauce from the stove and allow it to cool. In a baking dish, put down a layer of salmon, then a layer of sauce, then a layer of salmon, and so on. (I use a small loaf pan). Sprinkle the top with cracker crumbs and dot it with butter. Bake it for ½ an hour at 350° F.

SALMON ROLL

1 (15 ounce) can of salmon
¼ cup chopped onions
2 tablespoons chopped green pepper
2 tablespoons chopped celery
2 tablespoons catsup
½ teaspoon dry mustard
1 egg, beaten
Salt and pepper

Mix your own recipe for biscuit dough and roll it thin. Mix the salmon with the rest of the above ingredients and spread it on the dough, leaving a ½" margin. Roll the dough as if you were making a jelly roll, starting from the longest side. Moisten the edge of the dough and seal the roll. Place the salmon roll on a greased cookie sheet and fold the ends under. Bake it in a pre-heated oven at 450° F for 25 minutes. This roll may be served with an egg or cheese sauce.

SALMON IN BAKED POTATO SHELLS

1 pound canned salmon
8 medium-sized potatoes
½ cup milk
1 onion, chopped and simmer-
    ed in butter
1 cup dry bread crumbs
2 tablespoons butter

Bake the potatoes, slice off the tops, and scoop out the potato. Add the milk, the onions simmered in butter, salt, pepper, and salmon. Mix well. Put this mixture back in the potato shells, cover with crumbs, and dot with butter. Bake in a hot oven until they are brown — about 350° F for 25 minutes.

TAM-O'SHANTER SALMONBURGERS

    1 can (15½ ounces) salmon
    1 egg, beaten
    1 cup coarse, fresh bread crumbs
    ½ teaspoon salt
    1/8 teaspoon pepper
    2 tablespoons minced onion
    8 bacon strips
    8 hamburger buns, split
    8 slices tomato
    8 stuffed olives

Break up the salmon with a fork, crushing the soft bones and mixing them with the liquid. Add the bread crumbs, beaten egg, salt, pepper, and onion. Mix well. The mixture will be wet but not too difficult to handle. Shape it into 8 patties about the same diameter as the buns. Panfry the bacon strips; drain; keep them warm in a warm oven. Heat the buns.

Panfry the patties in about 1/8" of hot bacon fat over moderate heat. When brown on one side, turn them carefully and brown on the other side. Drain. Place a patty in each heated bun. Top with a slice of tomato and a strip of cooked bacon. Spear the stuffed olives with cocktail picks. Secure each bun lid with an olive pompom. Makes 8 hot snacks.

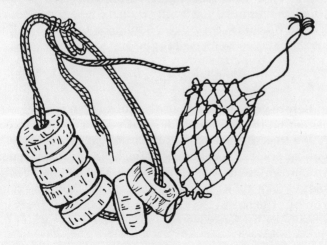

PICKLED HERRING

6 to 8 medium-sized salted herring
3 large bay leaves
½ teaspoon ground allspice
2 teaspoons whole allspice
5 white onions, sliced thin
2 cups white vinegar
¼ cup water
1¾ cups sugar
¼ teaspoon salt, pepper

Skin, bone, and soak the herring in very cold water. Wipe dry with paper towels. Cut the fish into 1" to 2" pieces; let them set in a pickle solution made with the above ingredients for 24-36 hours. Cover tightly.

For those interested, the above pickling solution also is great for pickling eggs. Cover as many hard-boiled eggs as possible with the pickle solution.

HOME-CANNED FISH

Most housewives today have a freezer for preserving food, but there is still considerable interest in canning. Canning fish can be successful as long as you are extremely careful about cleanliness, timing, and filling the bottles completely. Be certain to follow this rule: *Do not taste your home-canned fish until you have boiled or cooked it in an open dish for 10 to 15 minutes to destroy all toxins that may have formed in the jar.*

PROCESSING

Before you prepare your fish for the jars, place your canner on the stove and fill it with enough water to cover the tops of the jars. Let the water come almost to the boiling point. Prepare only enough fish to fill the jars you are going to have in the canner at one time. Fish should take about four hours — counted from the time you put the jars in the canner — to process properly. Always keep the jars covered with water. If the water boils down, add more.

PRE-COOKED FISH

Use firm, fresh fish that has been washed well and pre-cooked. Cut the fish up into conveniently-sized pieces and pack it in the jars. Leave 1 inch at the top. Add 1 teaspoon of salt per quart. Do not add water, since the fish makes its own juice. Work quickly, keeping the fish and jars hot so the jars will not break when put in the hot-water bath. Process the fish for four hours.

RAW FISH

Use fresh fish and do not remove the backbone. Cut it in large pieces and place it in brine, which is made by adding ½ pound salt to a gallon of water. Soak the fish from 10 minutes to an hour, depending on the size of the fish. Remove the fish from the brine and pack it in jars. Leave 1 inch at the top of the jars. Do not add water. Process for 4 hours.

FRIED FISH

Scale the fish and wash it in hot water. Cut it to the size you desire and dip it in either corn meal or cracker meal. Fry the fish until it is light brown. Pack it in clean jars. Leave 1 inch at the top of the jars. Add 1 teaspoon of salt per quart if you wish. Do not add water. Process for 4 hours.

CLAMS

Pre-cook the clams in mild salt water. Chop them or leave them whole, as you wish. Pack them in the jars, leaving 1 inch at the top. Cover the clams with a weak brine, which is made by adding 1 teaspoon of salt to 1 quart of water. Process for 4 hours.

SALMON

Clean the salmon, but scrape the skin gently so that there will be no loss of oil. Leave the backbone in and cut the fish into pieces. Pack the fish in jars to within 1 inch of the top. Add 1 teaspoon of salt and 1 tablespoon of olive oil per quart. Process for 4 hours.

TUNA

Steam or bake the tuna for about 1 hour. Remove the skin and bones. Pack the tuna into sterilized jars, leaving 1 inch at the top. Add 2 tablespoons of salad oil and ½ teaspoon of salt per pint. Process for 4 hours.

SHRIMP

Peel the shrimp and then cook it for 3 minutes in salted water. Pack it in sterilized jars, leaving 1 inch at the top. Add 1 teaspoon of salt to 2 tablespoons of the juice the shrimp were cooked in. Process for 4 hours.

FREEZING FISH

Only fresh fish should be frozen. The sooner you freeze it after it is caught, the better. Fatty fish, such as mackerel, tuna, and salmon should be cut into steaks or fillets and wrapped in freezer paper or plastic bags. Other fish is best when soaked in a saltwater brine for about 30 seconds, then dried and wrapped in freezer paper. The brine is made by adding 1 cup of salt to a gallon of water.

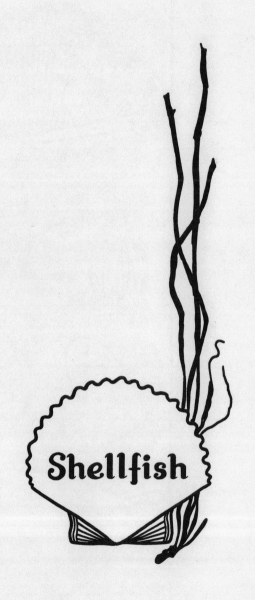

Shellfish

OYSTERS WILLIAMSBURG

2 containers (12 ounce each) medium-sized
    fresh oysters
½ cup ripe olives (or green pepper cut into
    small pieces)
1 tablespoon instant minced onion (or ¼
    cup finely chopped raw onion)
½ teaspoon paprika
½ teaspoon salt
¼ teaspoon ground pepper
1/8 teaspoon powdered garlic (or 1 finely
    chopped clove of garlic)
2 teaspoons Worcestershire sauce
2 tablespoons fresh lemon juice
½ cup margarine or butter
¾ cup sifted all-purpose flour
2 or 3 tablespoons cracker crumbs

*Cook the oysters in their own juice for several minutes
or until the edges curl. Cut up the olives into medium-
sized pieces and set them aside. Remove the oysters
from the liquid with a slotted spoon and set them aside.
Measure off 1½ cups of the oyster liquid; if there is not
enough, add chicken broth or water to make up the dif-
ference. To the oyster liquid, add the onion, paprika,
salt, pepper, garlic, Worcestershire sauce, and lemon
juice. In a separate pan, melt the margarine and stir in
the flour; cook over medium heat stirring constantly and
vigorously (the mixture will look like a paste at first but
will break down and thin out). Cook until it turns gold-
en brown, about 5 minutes. Remove it from the heat
and slowly stir the oyster liquid mixture into the browned mixture. Carefully fold in the oysters and olives (or
green pepper). Turn it into a 1½ quart casserole. Top
with crumbs. Bake in a hot oven 400° F for 30 minutes.
Makes 6 to 8 servings.*

OYSTER COCKTAIL

1 can (12 ounces) oysters,
  fresh or frozen
Lettuce
Cocktail sauce
Lemon wedges

If you are using frozen oysters, thaw them first. Drain off the liquid and place the oysters over lettuce that has been put in cocktail glasses. Top each serving with approximately ¼ cup of cocktail sauce. Serve the oyster cocktail with lemon wedges. This recipe serves 6.

COCKTAIL SAUCE

1 cup catsup
1 tablespoon finely chopped
  celery
1 tablespoon finely chopped
  onion
½ teaspoon salt
2 tablespoons lemon juice
1 tablespoon horseradish
1 teaspoon Worcestershire
  sauce
3 drops liquid hot pepper
  sauce

Combine all of the ingredients and mix them thoroughly. Chill the sauce. This recipe makes approximately 1 1/3 cups of sauce.

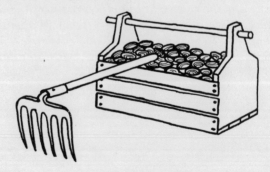

MANHATTAN ROAST OYSTERS

> 1 pint large oysters
> 1 1/8 cups fine dry bread
>   crumbs
> 1½ teaspoon salt
> Dash of pepper
> 1/3 cup butter, melted
> 1 egg, slightly beaten
> 1 tablespoon water
> ½ lemon
> Parsley

Drain the oysters thoroughly; combine the crumbs, salt, pepper, and melted butter. Roll the oysters in crumbs; then dip them in egg mixed with water, and roll again in crumbs. Arrange the oysters in a greased large shallow pan, one layer deep. Bake them in a hot oven 425° F for 15 to 20 minutes, or until the oysters are puffed and nicely browned. Serve with wedges of lemon and sprigs of parsley.

SCALLOPED OYSTERS

> 1 quart oysters, shucked and
>   washed
> 2 to 3 cups fresh soda cracker
>   crumbs, coarsely crushed
> ¼ pound butter or margarine
> 1 to 2 cups whole milk
> Salt and pepper

Drain the liquor from the oysters and reserve it. Grease a 2-quart casserole. Place alternate layers of oysters and crackers in the casserole, dotting each layer with butter or margarine and sprinkling it with salt and pepper. End with a layer of crumbs. Pour the milk and oyster liquor over all. Dot the top with more butter and bake the casserole at 350° F for 45 minutes to an hour.

BROILED OYSTERS
(Appetizers)

1 dozen large oysters, in shell
Worcestershire sauce
Tabasco sauce
1 strip bacon, finely chopped
Paprika

*Open the shells, letting the oyster remain in the curv-
ed half; discard the flatter half. Arrange the oysters in a
shallow baking pan. On each oyster put 1 to 2 drops of
Worcestershire and Tabasco sauce, 3 to 4 bits of bacon,
and a sprinkle of paprika. Place the oysters in a preheated broiler, 3 inches from the flame; broil them until
their edges curl and the bacon is done, 2 to 3 minutes.
This recipe makes 12 broiled oysters.*

ANGELS ON HORSEBACK

1 pint small oysters (canned
    oysters may also be used)
12 thin slices of side bacon

*Drain the oysters. Cut the bacon slices in half and
wrap each half around an oyster. Secure the bacon with
a toothpick. Place the wrapped oysters in a shallow
baking dish or on a broiler rack. Bake or broil them.
To broil them, put them about 4" from the top heat
until the bacon is crisp, turning once. Broiling time will
be about 7 minutes. To bake them, place them in a hot
oven (450° F). Baking time is 10 to 15 minutes, or until
the bacon is crisp.*

OYSTER STEW

1 pint shucked standard oysters
    with liquor
1 quart hot milk
¼ cup margarine or butter
Salt and pepper to taste
Paprika or parsley flakes to
    garnish

Cook the oysters in their liquor until the edges curl, about 5 minutes. Add the milk, margarine or butter, salt, and pepper. Heat the stew, but do not allow it to boil.

SCALLOPED OYSTERS

1 pint oysters
1 can mushroom soup
    (undiluted)
1½ cups crushed saltines
¼ pound butter

Heat the mushroom soup and melt the butter. Line a casserole with cracker crumbs, then a layer of oysters. Next add a layer of soup mixture and repeat again — ending with cracker crumbs. Bake at 425° F for 35 minutes.

STEAMED CLAMS

Soft-shell clams are used for steaming and should be bought in the shell if you do not dig them yourself. Always steam live clams; throw away dead ones, even those that appear to be borderline cases. Wash your clams in lukewarm water. This makes the clam open slightly, which will enable you to wash out all of the sand.

To steam clams, use about ½ cup of water for a 4-quart kettle of clams. Cover the kettle tightly and steam the clams for about 5 minutes from the time the water starts boiling, or until the shells are partially open. Put the clam broth in cups. Dip the clams into the broth and then into melted butter.

STEAMED MUSSELS

Blue mussels are excellent steamed. Europeans consider them one of the greatest delicacies. They are steamed in the same manner as clams. Vary your butter dip by putting a few drops of lemon juice or vinegar in the melted butter. You might even wish to add a little garlic to the butter.

RAW CLAMS

Cherrystone and littleneck clams are excellent on the half shell. Open the clams, throwing away one of the shells of each, and lay them on a dish of crushed ice. Serve them with lemon wedges and your favorite seafood cocktail sauce.

CLAM CHOWDER

2 cups shucked, steamed clams
   (or 2 cans of minced clams)
3 slices of uncooked bacon,
   diced (or ¼ pound butter)
1 large onion, chopped
2 cups clam liquor
3 large potatoes, diced
1 pint of milk
1 can of evaporated milk
2 tablespoons chopped parsley
1/8 teaspoon thyme
Salt and pepper to taste

   *Boil the potatoes, onion, bacon, and clam liquor
together until the potatoes are cooked. Add the
clams and cook for 2 minutes, then add the milk
(both types), parsley, thyme, salt, and pepper. Heat
the chowder thoroughly, but do not let it come to the
boiling point. Let it set for 1 hour, then reheat and
serve. Be sure that the milk does not boil.*
   *The larger of any type of clam is used for chowder.
Mud or sand clams make delicious chowders, since they
have white bellies.*

CLAM FRITTERS

2 cups sifted all-purpose flour
2½ teaspoons baking powder
1 teaspoon salt
¼ teaspoon pepper
1 egg, beaten
1 cup milk
2 tablespoons melted shortening
1 pint of clams

   *Sift all the dry ingredients together, then add the milk,
egg, and shortening. Drop a tablespoon of batter at a
time into a pan, and fry the fritters in butter until they
are browned on both sides.*

EASTERN SHORE CLAM BAKE

6 dozen clams
12 small onions
6 medium baking potatoes
6 ears of corn in husks
12 live blue crabs
Lemon wedges
Melted butter or margarine

Wash the clam shells thoroughly. Peel the onions and the potatoes, and then parboil them for 15 minutes; drain off the water. Remove the silk from the corn and replace the husks. Cut twelve 18"x36" pieces of heavy-duty aluminum foil. Put 2 pieces of cheesecloth on top of 2 pieces of aluminum foil. Place 2 onions, a potato, an ear of corn, 12 clams, and 2 crabs on the cheesecloth. Tie the cheesecloth up over the food. Cup the foil and pour 1 cup of water into the package. Bring the edges of the foil together and seal tightly. Make 5 more packages in the same manner. Put the packages on a barbecue grill about 4" from the hot coals. Cover them with a hood or aluminum foil. Cook them for 45 to 60 minutes, or until the onions and potatoes are done. Serve the clambake with lemon and butter.

MAINE CLAM CASSEROLE

2 cups clams, with juice
1 cup cracker crumbs
2 tablespoons chopped
   onions
3 eggs, slightly beaten
½ cup milk
½ cup cream style corn
2 tablespoons melted
   butter
Salt and pepper to taste

Combine all the ingredients and put the mixture into a buttered casserole. Bake for 45 to 60 minutes at 350° F. This casserole serves 4.

52

DEVILED CLAMS

2 cups clams
½ cup clam liquor
2 tablespoons minced onion
2 tablespoons minced green
   pepper
¼ cup chopped celery
4 tablespoons butter
1 teaspoon salt
1/8 teaspoon pepper
3 drops Tabasco sauce
½ teaspoon prepared mustard
¾ cup cracker crumbs

Chop the clams into fine pieces and simmer them in their liquor for 5 minutes. Cook the onion, green pepper, and celery in butter until they are tender; mix them with the clams and remaining ingredients. Put the mixture into ramekins or scallop shells, and bake in a moderate oven (350° F).

WHITE CLAM SAUCE

2 cans minced clams, drained
2 cloves garlic
2/3 cup oil
¼ cup sliced olives
¼ teaspoon salt
½ teaspoon pepper
1/3 cup chopped parsley
Grated cheese to taste

Drain the clams, reserving the liquor. Sauté the clams and garlic in oil for five minutes. Stir in the olives. Stir in the clam liquor, salt, and pepper. Simmer the sauce uncovered for 15 to 20 minutes. Add the parsley and mix well. Serve the sauce over hot spaghetti with grated cheese as a topping.

FRIED CLAMS

1 quart shucked, soft clams
   (steamers)
1 egg, beaten
1 tablespoon milk
1 teaspoon salt
Dash pepper
1 cup dry bread crumbs,
   cracker crumbs, or you
   may use 1 cup Quick
   Quaker Oats.

Drain the clams and wipe them dry. Combine the egg, milk, and seasonings. Dip the clams in the egg mixture and then roll them in the crumbs. Fry them in a basket in deep fat at 375° F for 2 to 3 minutes, or until golden brown. Drain the clams on an absorbent paper. Serve them plain, sprinkled with salt, or with sauce.

PUFFY CLAM BATTER

2 eggs
1 teaspoon salt
½ teaspoon pepper
1 cup flour
¾ cup milk
1 heaping teaspoon
   baking powder

This recipe is for those who would prefer a batter rather than an egg and crumb mixture to fry clams. Drain the clams and wipe them dry. Beat the eggs, and add the salt and pepper. Sift the flour and baking powder together, then add it alternately with the milk to the egg mixture to make a smooth batter. Fry the clams as in the preceding recipe.

CLAM BATTER

1 cup bread flour
½ teaspoon salt
Pepper to taste
2/3 cup milk
2 eggs, well beaten

Mix the dry ingredients, and pour the milk and eggs in slowly. Use this batter to cover the clams for deep frying at about 375° F.

CLAM CASSEROLE

2 cups clams with liquor
1 slice salt pork, diced
1 tablespoon fat
2 cups hot water
2 cups parboiled potatoes,
    diced
1 teaspoon salt
1/16 teaspoon pepper

Mix the clam liquor, hot water, pork, and fat. Simmer this mixture for 45 minutes. Add the salt, pepper, chopped clams, and diced potatoes. Place the mixture in a casserole. If you wish, a crust may be added. Bake this clam casserole in a hot oven for 20 minutes.

CLAM SANDWICH AU GRATIN

1 cup chopped clams
1 onion, diced
1 teaspoon prepared mustard
1 tablespoon mayonnaise

Mix the ingredients and spread the mixture thickly on thick slices of Italian bread (buttered). Top the sandwiches with grated cheese and place them under a broiler until the cheese melts. Dust the tops with paprika.

55

STUFFED CLAMS

2 dozen clams
6 fresh mushrooms, chopped
    fine
3 slices of cooked bacon,
    chopped fine
1 teaspoon minced parsley
Bread crumbs
Salt
Pepper

Remove the clams from the shells. Scrub the shells to remove all the sand and then sterilize them in boiling water. Combine the clams with the mushrooms, bacon, parsley, salt, and pepper. Add enough bread crumbs to this mixture so that it will hold its shape in the shells. Pack the stuffing in the clam shells, sprinkle with bread crumbs, and put a piece of butter on top. Bake the stuffed clams in a moderate oven (350° F) until they are brown on top, about 12 minutes.

CLAM STEW

1 pint of clams
¾ quart whole milk
1 small can evaporated milk
    or ½ pint of cream
½ teaspoon salt
Pepper to taste
4 tablespoons butter
Paprika

Grind the clams in a food chopper, saving the liquor. In a large saucepan, heat 2 tablespoons of butter, the milk, ½ cup clam liquor, and the salt. When the sauce is hot, add the clams, then heat the stew again. Just before serving, add the other 2 tablespoons of butter, the pepper, and the paprika.

SCALLOPED CLAMS

20 crackers (saltines)
1 quart plus 1 cup milk
1 quart clams (chopped
    fine)
Salt and pepper
Pieces of butter

Put the crackers through a food chopper. Mix the crackers, clams, and milk together. Add the butter, salt, and pepper. Bake this casserole in a hot oven for ¾ hour at 350° F. Served with toast and a sliced cucumber or tomato, it makes a very tasty lunch.

MOULES MARINIERES

12 dozen mussels
1 stalk celery (whole)
½ cup onions, chopped
Salt and pepper
½ pint white wine
1 cup Hollandaise sauce

Clean the mussels and put them in a large kettle with the celery, onions, salt, and pepper. Cover and steam them. When the mussels are open, discard one shell of each. Place the mussels in a casserole and cover them. Pour the liquid from the kettle slowly into a saucepan, leaving behind any sand. Add wine to the liquid and briskly stir in Hollandaise sauce. Heat the sauce (do not boil) and pour it over the mussels. Serve the moules marinieres very hot.

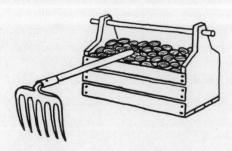

CRUSTY SCALLOPS

2 pounds sea scallops, fresh or
     frozen
1 medium onion, quartered
10 salted crackers
2 medium potatoes, cooked
2 eggs
½ cup flour, divided
1/8 teaspoon pepper
¼ cup cornmeal

If the scallops are frozen, defrost them. Cover them
with cold, salted water and bring them to a boil; simmer
them for 3 minutes and then drain them. Put the scallops through a food chopper with a coarse knife, alter-
nating with the onions, crackers, and potatoes. Combine the chopped foods with the eggs, ¼ cup flour, and
pepper; mix them well. Shape this mixture into small
croquettes. Combine the remaining flour and cornmeal
and sprinkle the mixture over the croquettes. Fry the
croquettes in shallow fat (1½" deep) heated to 375°F
for about 2 minutes; turn them to brown on the other
side. Drain them on absorbent paper and serve them
with tartar sauce. This recipe makes 6 servings.

FRIED SCALLOPS

1 pound of scallops
1 egg, beaten
1 cup crushed cracker crumbs
     or fine bread crumbs

Cover the scallops with boiling water and let them
stand for 3 minutes; drain and dry them with a paper
towel. Dip the scallops in egg, then in crumbs, and fry
them in oil or fat until they are golden brown. Some-
times I bake them about 15 minutes at 450°F. (You
have to turn them to brown.)

SCALLOP STEW

1 pint scallops, chopped in
    pieces
1 quart milk
1 can evaporated milk or
    1 cup cream
½ teaspoon salt
¼ teaspoon pepper
¼ pound butter
Paprika

Melt the butter in a pan and sauté the scallops until they are no longer translucent. Add the scallops to the milk and heat all in a 2-quart kettle. Add the salt, pepper, and paprika. Do not let the stew come to a boil — just heat it until it is scalded. You will find the stew has a better flavor if it is reheated before it is served.

SCALLOP CAKES

1 pint of scallops
2 eggs
2 cups flour
2 teaspoons baking powder
Milk
Salt
Pepper

Parboil the scallops in very little water; drain off the water and chop them very fine. Beat the eggs slightly, then add the flour sifted with baking powder. Mix this with enough milk to make a batter that will drop easily from a spoon. Beat the batter well and add the scallops. Heat ½ cup cooking oil in a frying pan and drop the batter by spoonfuls into the hot oil. Sprinkle the top with seasonings. Brown the cakes and turn them to brown on the other side.

CURRIED SCALLOPS IN
PEPPER SHELL

1 pound scallops, fresh or frozen
6 green peppers
1 cup boiling water
1 teaspoon salt
2 eggs, beaten
3 tablespoons grated onion
1 teaspoon celery salt
1 teaspoon curry powder
2 tablespoons chopped pimento
Dash cayenne pepper
2 tablespoons butter or margarine,
    melted
½ cup dry bread crumbs

*If the scallops are frozen, thaw them. Remove any
shell particles and wash the scallops. Chop them up.
Cut the peppers in half lengthwise and remove the seeds.
Wash the peppers; cook them in boiling water for 12 to
15 minutes. Drain off the water. Combine the egg,
onion, seasonings, and the scallops. Fill the peppers and
place them in a baking pan 11"x7"x1". Combine the
butter and crumbs. Sprinkle this over the tops of the
peppers. Bake the scallops in a moderate oven (350°F)
for 25 to 30 minutes, or until they are brown. This
recipe serves 6.*

SCALLOPED SCALLOPS

1 pint scallops, washed and sliced
1 cup cracker crumbs
1½ cup soft bread crumbs
½ cup butter

*Mix the cracker crumbs, bread crumbs, and butter.
Put a layer of the crumb mixture in a buttered baking
dish and cover it with a layer of scallops. Add 3 tablespoons of cream. Repeat the layers and cover the top
with the remaining crumbs. Bake the scallops for 25
minutes at 375°F.*

60

SCALLOPS BAKED IN SHELLS

1 pound scallops
Salt
Pepper
4 tablespoons heavy cream
4 teaspoons fine dry bread
    crumbs
4 teaspoons melted butter

Place four or five scallops in each of four greased scallop shells or custard cups. Season them with salt and pepper, and add one tablespoon of cream to each shell or baking dish. Top each dish with one teaspoon of melted butter. Bake the scallops in a hot oven. This makes 4 servings.

SCALLOPS PORTUGUESE

1 pound Cape or sea scallops
¼ cup butter or margarine
1 garlic clove, minced
½ teaspoon salt
Few grains pepper
½ cup chopped parsley

If you use sea scallops, cut them in half. Pat them dry with paper toweling. Melt the butter or margarine. Add the garlic and salt; cook the garlic until it is a golden brown. Add the scallops; then cook them 5 to 7 minutes, stirring often. Sprinkle them with freshly ground black pepper, add the freshly chopped parsley, and cook them for 1 minute longer. Serve the scallops hot. Makes 8 servings.

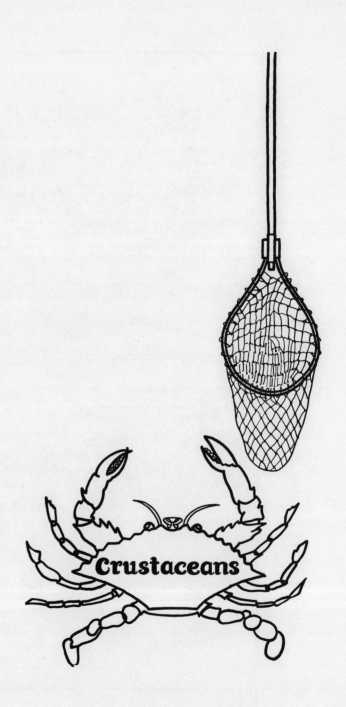

Crustaceans

RICE

MBS

COOKING AND FREEZING SHRIMP

The following steps do not necessarily apply to all shrimp. They work best with the small variety, such as the Maine shrimp.

Wash the shrimp and remove the heads. If you cook shrimp with the heads still on, you might notice a strong iodine taste. Put the shrimp in a pan for cooking. If you are working with a large quantity, you might want to use a canner. Put 1 inch of water in the bottom of the pan, as shrimp taste best when steamed. Steam the shrimp for about 3 minutes from the time the water starts boiling. The shrimp should be pink and no longer translucent. Cool the shrimp in iced brine (1 teaspoon salt to 1 cup of ice water), then remove them from the shell by pinching the meat out, starting at the tail. Some of the shrimp will have to be de-veined and some will not; small shrimp do not have a prominent sand vein. You will notice, when removing the shrimp from the shells, that some of the roe will adhere to the meat. I merely rinse it off, and then put the shrimp in 1-pound baggies before freezing.

SHRIMP AND PEAS ON CRACKERS

> 2 tablespoons butter
> 2 tablespoons flour
> 1 cup milk
> 1 cup cooked shrimp
> 1 cup frozen peas,
>   thawed
> Salt, pepper, and paprika
>   to taste

Melt the butter in a saucepan; stir in the flour and salt. Add the milk and cook the same until it is thickened, stirring constantly. Now add the shrimp and peas, and heat until the peas are done. Serve this sauce over crackers. You will find that most children think this dish is extra-special.

CREAMED SHRIMP

1 pint of shrimp
1 cup of cream
½ cup of milk
1 heaping tablespoon of
    flour
1 tablespoon of salt
1 tablespoon of butter
1 cracker
1 tablespoon of Worcester-
    shire sauce
Dash of cayenne
1 cup cooked, frozen peas

Put the shrimp into the cream and heat. Mix the milk and flour, and add them to the hot cream with the other ingredients. Thicken the sauce, and add one cup cooked frozen peas. This may be served over crackers or toast.

SHRIMP CASSEROLE

1 can shrimp
½ cup grated cheese
1/3 cup fine bread crumbs
1 cup frozen peas
¾ cup canned carrots
1 onion, diced
¾ cup salt
2 eggs, beaten
1½ cups milk
Salt, pepper, paprika to taste

Mix all of the ingredients and place them in a well-greased baking dish. Set the baking dish in a pan of hot water in the oven and bake the casserole for 1 hour at 350° F.

SHRIMP JAMBALAYA

2 cups fresh or frozen shrimp
   or 2 cans (4½ ounces)
½ cup diced ham
2 tablespoons butter, melted
½ cup chopped onion
1 cup chopped green pepper
2 cloves garlic, finely chopped
1½ cups canned tomatoes
1½ cups water
1 cup uncooked rice
¼ teaspoon salt
1 bay leaf
½ teaspoon crushed whole thyme
Dash cayenne pepper
¼ cup chopped parsley

Drain the shrimp; if frozen, thaw it. Cook the ham in butter for 3 minutes. Add the onion, green pepper, and garlic, and cook them until tender. Add the tomatoes, liquid, rice, and seasonings. Cover the mixture and cook it for 25 to 30 minutes, or until the rice is tender. Stir constantly. Add the parsley and shrimp, and heat. This recipe serves 6. Be sure to use the specified seasonings — they provide the unique flavor of shrimp jambalaya.

SHRIMP AND PINEAPPLE SALAD

2 cups fresh, cooked shrimp,
   de-veined
          or
2 cans shrimp
1 cup pineapple, crushed
1 pint cottage cheese

Mix the shrimp and pineapple together and serve them on lettuce leaves arranged around a mound of cottage cheese. Juice from the pineapple makes enough dressing for the salad. This makes an excellent lunch when served with crackers and coffee.

67

TEMPURA

2 pounds large raw shrimp in shells
2 pounds halibut steaks, ½" thick
1 large onion
1 large green pepper
   Batter:
3 eggs, beaten
Ice water (about 3 cups)
All-purpose flour (about 3¾ cups)

Shell the shrimp, leaving the tail fins attached to the flesh. Make a shallow cut lengthwise down the back of each shrimp and wash out the sand vein. Dry them thoroughly. Make several shallow cuts across the belly side of each shrimp to prevent curling during frying. Cut the halibut into pieces about 1" by 2". Wash and dry the vegetables. Cut the onion into slices about ¼" thick, then halve the slices and skewer them with toothpicks. Cut the green pepper lengthwise into ¼" strips.

To prepare the batter, measure the volume of the beaten eggs, then measure out four times their volume in water and five times their volume in flour. Combine the eggs and water, then add the flour all at once, mixing it in lightly with two or three stirs. A French whip is ideal for mixing. Dip the prepared foods into the batter, holding the shrimp by their tails and the other foods with tongs or chop sticks.

Cook the foods in deep, hot vegetable oil preheated to 350°F. Deep-fry only a few pieces at a time to avoid cooling the oil. The foods cook rapidly, the vegetables taking only about 1 minute and the halibut and shrimp 2 to 3 minutes. When cooked, the coating will be a pale golden shade and crisp. Remove and drain the foods on paper towels. Skim any stray bits of batter from the oil after each batch is cooked.

Tempura is best served immediately, but to hold, keep it on a paper-towel-lined cookie sheet in a warm oven. Serve a combination of seafood and vegetables to each guest along with a small bowl containing ¼ to 1/3 cup of dipping sauce. This recipe makes 8 servings.

DIPPING SAUCE

2 chicken bouillon cubes
2 cups boiling water
½ cup soy sauce
2½ tablespoons sugar
½ cup sherry (optional)
1/8 teaspoon monosodium glutamate
    (or a paste of 2 tablespoons flour
    using ½ cup of the water to be
    boiled as a thickening agent)

Dissolve the bouillon cubes in the boiling water. Add the other ingredients and mix them well. Serve the sauce warm in individual small bowls. This sauce serves 8.

SHRIMP AND CHEESE OMELET

4 eggs, beaten
Salt and pepper to taste
3 tablespoons milk
¼ cup finely shaved cheese
1 cup (or 1 can) shrimp,
    cut up
Cooking oil (a scant teaspoon)

Beat the eggs and milk together, and add the salt and pepper. Pour this mixture into a heated frying pan to which oil has been added and cook it over a low heat on one side. When it is slightly browned on that side, cut the omelet into four sections and turn them even though they are runny. After they have been turned, the 4 sections will meld together into 1 piece again. Pour the shaved or grated cheese over the eggs with the shrimp. When cooked on the other side, fold the omelet together and turn off the heat. This is usually enough for three people.

SHRIMP AND RICE CASSEROLE

1½ cups shrimp, cooked (canned
    may be used)
1 cup cooked rice
¼ cup minced onion
1 tablespoon parsley flakes
1 tablespoon green pepper,
    chopped
2 tablespoons melted butter
¼ teaspoon salt
¼ teaspoon pepper
1 can (10 ounce) cream of
    mushroom soup
½ cup milk
2 cups potato chips
¼ cup cashews, crushed

*Mix the shrimp and rice. Cook the onion, green pep-
per, and parsley in melted butter over a low heat until
they are tender; add the salt and pepper and fold into
the shrimp mixture. Add the soup and milk to the mixture also. Now place half the potato chips in a greased
1½ quart casserole and cover them with the shrimp mixture, to which the soup and milk have already been added. Top this with the remaining potato chips and crushed cashews. Bake the casserole uncovered in a moderate
oven for about 35 minutes at 400° F.*

SHRIMP AND WILD RICE CASSEROLE

2 boxes long grain wild rice
1 (10½ ounce) can cream of
    chicken soup
¾ cup dry white wine or water
2 (4 ounce) cans sliced mush-
    rooms, drained
1 pound cooked shrimp

*Cook the rice according to the package directions.
Stir in the soup and wine and heat thoroughly. Fold in
the mushrooms and shrimp. Place the mixture in a
casserole and garnish it with parsley. Serve.*

SHRIMP PIZZA

1 cup milk
1 cup hot water
3 tablespoons sugar
1 teaspoon salt
2 packages dry yeast
4 tablespoons shortening
6 cups flour, unsifted
Vegetable or olive oil
1 can spaghetti sauce
Chopped onions
Small chopped shrimp
Mushrooms
Pimento cheese
Summer savory
Salt and pepper

*Make a plain roll dough from 1 cup of hot water, 1
cup milk, 3 tablespoons sugar, 1 teaspoon salt, 2 packages dry yeast, and 4 tablespoons of melted shortening.
Mix all these ingredients together and add 6 cups of unsifted flour. Be sure the yeast dissolves well before the
flour is added. Let this dough rise for 2 hours and then
cut it in three pieces. Two pieces may be placed in the
refrigerator for future use, but should be used within 3*

*To make 3 pizzas, roll each piece of dough thin enough
to fill a cookie sheet. Grease the sheet first. Put the
dough on and spread it with vegetable or olive oil. Then
use a can of spaghetti sauce — with meat is the best. The
contents will cover all 3 pizzas. Now add chopped
onions and lots of small shrimp (canned or fresh). I put
mushrooms — the bits and pieces — on also. Then cover
the shrimp as much as possible with pimento cheese.
The flavor is improved if you sprinkle on summer savory,
salt, and pepper. Put the pizza in the oven and let it
bake for about 12 minutes at 475° F. Be sure that the
bottom of the crust is cooked before you take it out.
I notice that on different stoves, I have to vary the time
considerably.*

SHRIMP JAMBALAYA

1 cup rice
2 tablespoons butter
1 tablespoon fat
1 tablespoon flour
1 pound ham, cooked and
  chopped
1 cup cooked shrimp
1½ cups cooked tomatoes
1 onion, sliced
¼ teaspoon thyme
1 clove garlic, crushed
1 green pepper, chopped
1 tablespoon minced parsley
Salt, pepper, and paprika
1 teaspoon Worcestershire
  sauce

Cook 1 cup of rice as directed on the package. When it is cooked and fluffy, add 2 tablespoons of butter. Set the rice aside. In a large, heavy frying pan, melt the fat and add the flour, stirring until it is smooth and slightly brown. Add the chopped ham, shrimp, tomatoes, and onion. Cook this for 3 minutes and then add the seasonings. Add this mixture to the rice and pour it all in a buttered pan. Sprinkle the top with a few cracker crumbs. Bake this for about 30 minutes at 425° F, or until the crumbs are well browned.

For added enjoyment, try using a package of seasoned wild rice. Prepare it as directed on the package and, when it is cooked, pour it over a mound of freshly boiled small shrimp. The flavor cannot be matched. Even canned, rather than fresh, shrimp can be used.

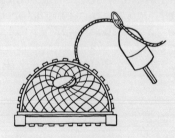

SHRIMP TARTS

½ cup butter or shortening
3 ounces cream cheese
1 cup pastry flour
2 tablespoons cream
½ slice pimento cheese
¼ cup small cooked shrimp

Work the butter and cream cheese into the flour. Add the cream, and chill. Roll the dough thin and cut it like turnovers. Fill the dough with ½ slice pimento cheese and about ¼ cup small shrimp. Bake at 400° F for 15 to 20 minutes.

SHRIMP TURNOVERS

½ pound cooked, peeled, cleaned
    shrimp, fresh or frozen
        or
2 cans (4½ ounces each) shrimp
2 tablespoons lemon juice
3 tablespoons mayonnaise or
    salad dressing
1 tablespoon chopped sweet pickle
1 teaspoon horseradish
1 teaspoon prepared mustard
1 teaspoon salt
1 cup or 1 stick pastry mix
Milk

Thaw the frozen shrimp or drain the canned shrimp. Grind the shrimp. Combine all the ingredients except the pastry mix; blend them into a paste. Prepare the pastry mix as directed. Roll it very thin and cut it into 2-inch circles. Place 1 teaspoon of filling in the center of each circle. Moisten the edges with cold water, fold them over, and press the edges together with a fork. Place the turnovers on a cooky sheet 15"x12". Prick the tops and brush them with milk. Bake the turnovers in a very hot oven (475° F) for 12 to 15 minutes, or until golden brown. This recipe makes approximately 48 turnovers.

PICKLED SHRIMP WITH
MUSTARD SAUCE

2 pounds cleaned, cooked shrimp
½ cup minced parsley
1 onion, minced
1 clove garlic, minced
¼ cup salad oil
1/3 cup white wine vinegar
1 teaspoon salt

*Place the shrimp in a large wide-mouth jar and pour
the rest of the ingredients over them. Leave the shrimp
for 3 hours before serving. (A day or two is better as
the shrimp improve after marinating.)*

CHINESE MUSTARD SAUCE

1/3 cup dry mustard
1 tablespoon salad oil
1 teaspoon sugar
½ teaspoon salt
2 tablespoons water or wine

*Mix the ingredients, in the order given, in a small serv-
ing bowl. This makes an excellent shrimp dip.*

DEVILED EGGS IN SHRIMP SAUCE

12 deviled egg halves
1 can (10 ounce) frozen
    condensed cream of
    shrimp soup
½ soup can of milk
Oven-buttered toast points

*Prepare the deviled eggs using your favorite recipe.
Combine the soup and milk. Heat until the soup is
thawed; stir often. Place the eggs filled side up in soup.
Cover; simmer until eggs are hot. For each serving,
place 3 egg halves on toast points. Pour the soup over
them. This recipe makes 4 servings.*

SHRIMP-CRAB CASSEROLE

1½ pounds shrimp
½ pound crab meat
½ green pepper, chopped
½ cup parsley, chopped
2 cups cooked rice
1½ cups mayonnaise
1½ to 2 packages frozen
    peas, thawed
Salt and pepper, to taste

Combine all the ingredients as listed; toss them lightly. Place the mixture in a greased casserole. Cover the casserole and bake for 45 minutes to 1 hour at 350° F.

OPEN-FACED SHRIMP SANDWICH

Toast a hamburger bun and brush it with melted butter. Put 1 cup of shrimp (or less) over one-half of the bun. Put lettuce with a dab of mayonnaise over the other half. Serve the sandwich with sliced tomatoes and potato chips. This makes a delicious lunch.

POTATO-SHRIMP SALAD

6 boiled, cold potatoes (medium
    sized)
2 cans shrimp or 1 pound fresh,
    boiled shrimp
1 onion, diced
6 hard-boiled eggs
½ head of lettuce
½ cup of mayonnaise
Green olives

Cube the potatoes and add the diced onion, mayonnaise, and drained shrimp. Line a large platter with lettuce leaves and spread them with the potato mixture, which has been mixed with mayonnaise. Slice the eggs and garnish the potato mixture with a circle of slices. Dot the mixture with sliced green olives.

SHRIMP CHRISTMAS TREE

3 pounds shrimp, fresh or frozen
2 quarts water
½ cup salt
4 large bunches curly endive
1 Styrofoam cone, 2½' high
1 Styrofoam square, 12"x12"x1"
1 small box round toothpicks
Cocktail sauce

Thaw the shrimp if frozen. Place the shrimp in boiling, salted water. Cover them and allow to simmer about 5 minutes, or until the shrimp are pink and tender. Drain off the water and peel the shrimp, leaving the last section of the shell on. Remove the sand veins and wash the shrimp. Chill. Separate and wash the endive. Chill.

Place a cone in the center of the Styrofoam square and draw a circle around the base of the cone. Cut out the circle and insert the cone. Cover the base and cone with overlapping leaves of endive. Fasten the endive to the Styrofoam with toothpick halves. Start at the outside edge of the base and work up. Cover the cone fully with greens to make it resemble a Christmas tree. Attach the shrimp to the tree with toothpicks. Provide a cocktail sauce for dunking.

SHRIMP BOATS

½ pound cheddar cheese, grated
¼ pound butter
½ cup salad dressing
2 tablespoons lemon juice
2 tablespoons onion juice
2 (7 ounce) cans shrimp or 2
    cups fresh-cooked shrimp
Hot dog rolls

Combine all of the ingredients and mix them together. Fill the rolls with the mixture and bake them for 20 minutes at 350° F.

76

SHRIMP CHOWDER

2 cups fresh shrimp (or canned)
1 small onion, chopped fine
2 cups diced, raw potatoes
2 tablespoons butter
¼ teaspoon salt
2 pints scalded milk
1 cup boiling water (if canned
    shrimp are used, use ½ cup
    water and ½ cup shrimp juice)
Pepper
Celery salt

Cook the onion and potatoes in boiling water — add the shrimp when the potatoes are soft — if fresh shrimp are used, cook 1 more minute; if canned, immediately add the milk and seasonings. Let the chowder set for ½ hour. Reheat to scalding temperature and serve. (Do not boil.)

LOBSTER

Lobster is at its best when steamed. Steaming preserves the flavor, and the goodness is not washed down the drain. Your live lobsters should be put in a steamer with very little water and covered tightly. Add 1 teaspoon of salt for each lobster. Steam them for about 30 minutes, or until they are red and one of the feelers pulls out easily. If you wish to boil your lobster, just plunge it into boiling water and cook for 20 minutes.

Always buy your lobster live. A live lobster is green and active; when cooked, its color changes to red. Some people prefer their lobster with just plain melted butter, and others prefer it in salads, in sandwiches, or baked. If you are preparing the lobster to eat after steaming or boiling, use the following steps:

1. Twist off the claws and crack them with a nutcracker.

2. Separate the tail and bend it backwards until it breaks. Use a fork to push the meat out. Remove the vein; this black vein is not edible.

3. Remove the tomalley liver from the body and eat it on crackers. It's a green color and delicious. If you find a red coral cluster in the lobster, it makes excellent eating too.

4. Use a nut pick to pick out the meat in the body after you have separated it. You will also find delicious meat in the tiny legs.

BAKED STUFFED LOBSTERS

2 live 1-pound lobsters
2 cups soft bread cubes
2 tablespoons butter or
    margarine, melted
1 tablespoon grated onion
Dash garlic salt

Place the lobster on its back and insert a sharp knife between the body and shell and tail segment, cutting down to sever the spinal cord. Cut the lobster in half lengthwise. Remove the stomach, which is just in back of the head, and the intestinal vein, which runs from the stomach to the tip of the tail. Remove and save the green liver and coral roe. Crack the claws.

Combine the bread cubes, butter, onion, green liver, and coral roe. Place this mixture in the body cavity and spread it over the surface of the tail meat. Sprinkle the top with paprika. Place the lobsters on a baking pan 15½"x10½"x1". Bake them in a hot oven (400° F) for 20 minutes, or until they are lightly browned.

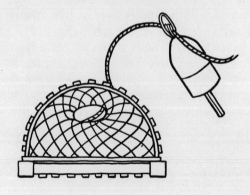

LOBSTER NEWBURG

2 cups boiled lobster meat
¼ teaspoon salt
¼ teaspoon white pepper
¼ teaspoon paprika
2 tablespoons butter
½ ounce brandy
½ cup sherry
1 pint of heavy cream
Toast

Season the lobster pieces with salt, white pepper, and paprika. (White pepper gives extra flavor, but black pepper will do.) Melt the butter in a saucepan, then fry the lobster pieces gently for about 2 minutes. Add the brandy and the sherry. Let this simmer until the liquid is reduced by half. Add the cream. Let it simmer again until creamy. Add the remaining butter, but do not allow the lobster to boil. Serve the lobster newburg over freshly made toast.

LOBSTER-STUFFED PEPPERS

4 medium green peppers
1 can lobster
¼ teaspoon salt
1/8 teaspoon pepper
1 cup white sauce
2 tablespoons chili sauce
2 hard-cooked eggs, chopped
1 cup buttered bread crumbs

Wash the peppers, cut off the stem ends, and remove the insides. Parboil the peppers for five minutes. Combine all the ingredients except the bread crumbs. Mix this stuffing well and fill it in the peppers. Sprinkle the top liberally with bread crumbs. Place the peppers in a baking dish and add 1 cup of hot water around them. Bake the peppers in a 400° F oven for 35 minutes. These are delicious served with rice and frozen peas.

SHELLFISH SALAD

1 can crabmeat
1 can lobster
1 can shrimp
6 radishes
1 avocado, diced
1 cucumber, peeled, marked with
   fork, and sliced
2 hard-boiled eggs, sliced
Mayonnaise to taste
Paprika
½ head of lettuce

Break the lettuce up and place the pieces on a platter. Mix all the ingredients together except the cucumber. Place the mixture in a mound on the lettuce. Surround it with the cucumber slices. Sprinkle the top with paprika. Radish rosettes can be placed in the center for decoration.

LOBSTER CUTLETS

1 can lobster
4 egg yolks
1 tablespoon butter
Juice of 1 lemon
1 cup milk
Salt
2 tablespoons flour
1 tablespoon freshly chopped
   parsley
1 teaspoon chopped onion
Pepper

To 1 can of lobster, add the juice of 1 lemon. Stir and let the lobster marinate for 30 minutes. Make a cream sauce with the egg yolks, milk, flour, butter, salt, pepper, onion, and parsley. Cook the sauce until it is thick, then add it to the lobster. Allow the lobster to cool. Shape the lobster into cutlets, dip them in egg and cracker crumbs, and fry. Serve the lobster cutlets with fish sauce.

MOCK LOBSTER CASSEROLE

½ pint light cream
½ cup milk
2 tablespoons flour
Scant ½ teaspoon mustard
1 teaspoon salt and paprika
¾ pound king crab meat (or
    lobster meat) cut in pieces
4 slices bread cut in cubes

Mix the ingredients together; top with cornflakes and dot with butter. Bake the casserole for ½ hour in a 375° F oven.

LOBSTER NEWBURG

3 tablespoons margarine
3 tablespoons flour
½ teaspoon salt
1½ cups milk
2 cups cooked, chopped
    lobster pieces
1 cup sliced celery
2 tablespoons chili sauce
2 teaspoons lemon juice
Dash paprika
Parsley or olive slices

Melt the margarine in a saucepan, and blend in the flour and salt. Remove the pan from the heat. Gradually add the milk, stirring until the mixture is smooth. Cook the sauce over a medium heat, stirring constantly until the mixture comes to a boil. Reduce the heat and simmer the sauce for 1 minute. Add the lobster, celery, chili sauce, lemon juice, and paprika. Heat. Serve the lobster newburg over rice, garnished with sprigs of parsley, olive slices, etc.

NEPTUNE'S NEWBURG

¾ pound cooked lobster meat
¼ cup butter or margarine
2 tablespoons flour
1 teaspoon salt
¼ teaspoon paprika
Dash cayenne pepper
1 pint coffee cream
2 egg yolks, beaten
2 tablespoons sherry
Toast points

Cut the lobster meat into ½-inch pieces. Melt the butter and blend in the flour and seasonings. Add the cream gradually and cook the same until it is thick and smooth, stirring constantly. Stir a little of the hot sauce into the egg yolks and add this to the remaining sauce, stirring constantly. Add the lobster meat and heat. Remove the sauce from the heat and slowly stir in the sherry. Serve this newburg immediately on toast points. This recipe serves 6.

LOBSTER LOAF

1 can lobster (6 ounce)
1 cup soft bread crumbs
1 can corn
2 eggs slightly beaten
½ cup milk
1 tablespoon onion, grated
2 tablespoons chopped pickle
Salt and pepper to taste

Drain the lobster and combine it with the bread crumbs and corn. Beat the eggs slightly and add the milk to them. Combine the two mixtures. Add the onion, pickles, and seasonings to taste. Turn the mixture into a greased loaf pan and bake it at 350° F for 40 minutes.

MOCK LOBSTER SALAD

2 pounds fillet of haddock
1 stalk celery
1 teaspoon salt
1½ cups boiling water
½ tablespoon paprika
1/8 teaspoon pepper
¼ cup French dressing
Celery salt
Lettuce
Mayonnaise

Cook the fish and celery in boiling water until they are tender (about 10 minutes). Drain off the water and remove the celery and flaked fish. Sprinkle the top with French dressing and paprika. Serve the fish on lettuce with mayonnaise.

NEPTUNE CASSEROLE

4 pounds lobster, crab meat,
    or shrimp
2 medium cans mushrooms
2 tablespoons olive oil
2 medium cans peas
1 large onion
2 tablespoons lemon juice

Cut the lobster, crab meat, or shrimp (depending on personal preference) into bite-size chunks. Add the mushrooms, peas, and onion rings; mix thoroughly. Sauté this mixture in olive oil over a moderate flame. Before serving, sprinkle this dish with lemon juice for a new, stimulating flavor. Serve in a casserole dish. This recipe yields 6 to 8 servings.

STEAMED CRABS

Place your live crabs (about 10 of them) in a large pot and cover them tightly so they will not escape. Pour over the crabs 2 cups of cider vinegar and 1 cup of water mixed with salt, pepper, celery salt, mustard, and any other seasonings you desire. Put the cover back on the pot and turn on the heat. The crabs are done when they turn red or when their aprons are loose. The time is about 25 to 30 minutes. Remove them from the fire and allow them to cool. Prepare them for eating as follows:

A mallet and knife are used. The first step is to pry off the apron flap on the underside and discard it. Then lift off the top shell and throw it away; break off the claws and set them aside for eating. There are 3 triangular membrane pieces, which should be scraped off to expose the edible crabmeat underneath. Next break the body in half. Finding the edible meat is easy, but you really need the mallet. Steamed crabs are excellent served with cold drinks and salad. Almost everyone serves them with hot pepper seasoning, which makes a beverage imperative.

CRAB MEAT PANCAKES

1 pound king crab meat
1½ cups white sauce

Add enough paprika to the white sauce to make it pink. Fill the pancakes with crab meat. Roll them and cover them with white sauce.

CRAB CANAPES

1 cup crab meat, flaked
10 ripe olives, minced
½ teaspoon Worcestershire sauce

Mix the crab flakes with the olives and Worcestershire sauce. Spread the mixture on prepared toast diamonds. Broil the canapes for 2 minutes and serve them hot.

84

KING CRAB FRUIT SALAD

¾ pound king crab meat or other
    crab meat, fresh or frozen, or
2 cans (6½ ounces each) crab meat
3 oranges
1 avocado
1 tablespoon orange juice
Lettuce
Orange dressing

If you are using frozen crab meat, thaw it. Drain the crab meat and remove any remaining shell or cartilage. Peel and section the oranges, reserving the juice. Cut the avocado in half lengthwise and remove the seed. Peel and slice the avocado, and then sprinkle it with orange juice to prevent discoloration. Place the lettuce on salad plates. Arrange the avocado slices and orange sections in a pinwheel on the lettuce. Place ¼ cup of crab meat in the center of the fruit. Top each serving with approximately 1 tablespoon of orange dressing. This recipe serves 6.

ORANGE DRESSING

1/3 cup mayonnaise or salad
    dressing
1 tablespoon orange juice
2 tablespoons catsup
1½ teaspoons grated orange rind
½ teaspoon lemon juice

Combine all the ingredients and mix them thoroughly. Chill. This recipe makes approximately ½ cup of dressing.

CRABMEAT AND AVOCADO SALAD

3 or 4 avocados
Lemon juice
½ pound fresh crabmeat
2 stalks celery
½ teaspoon celery salt
Salt

Slice the avocados in half and remove the large seeds. Peel the avocados and rub them with lemon juice inside and out to prevent them from turning brown. Fill them with a mixture of ½ pound of fresh, cooked crabmeat mixed with two stalks of celery and ½ teaspoon of celery salt. Before filling the avocados, salt them a little. Place the avocado cups on lettuce leaves and pour French dressing over the crabmeat. This salad should be chilled for about ½ hour.

CRAB AU GRATIN

1 can crabmeat
½ cup sharp cheddar cheese,
   grated
1 tablespoon sherry
White bread

Toast one side only of the white bread slices. Butter the untoasted sides and spread them with crabmeat. Sprinkle the crabmeat thickly with grated cheese and broil it until the cheese is melted. A moment before removing it from the broiler, pour on sherry. Serve this dish at once.

FRIED SOFT SHELL CRABS

Wash the crabs and dry them thoroughly. Season them lightly with salt and pepper; roll them in flour. Fry the crabs in deep, hot fat. Dry them on paper towels and serve with lemon wedges or tartar sauce. Note: Watch the crabs carefully, as they brown quickly.

CRABMEAT QUICKIE

3 cups cooked rice
1 can crabmeat
2 cups white sauce
1 can mushrooms
1 can whole kernel corn

Combine all the ingredients, and sprinkle the top with cheese. Bake this dish at 350° F for 30 minutes.

DEVILED CRAB

1 pound crab meat, fresh or
   pasteurized
2 tablespoons onion
2 tablespoons melted fat or oil
2 tablespoons flour
¾ cup milk
1 tablespoon lemon juice
1½ teaspoons powdered mustard
1 teaspoon Worcestershire sauce
½ teaspoon salt
3 drops liquid hot pepper sauce
Dash pepper
Dash cayenne pepper
1 egg, beaten
1 tablespoon chopped parsley
1 tablespoon melted fat or oil
¼ cup dry bread crumbs

Remove any remaining shell or cartilage from the crab meat. Cook the onion in fat until it is tender. Blend in the flour. Add the milk gradually and cook the sauce until it is thick, stirring constantly. Add the lemon juice and seasonings. Stir a little of the hot sauce into the egg; add this to the remaining sauce, stirring constantly. Add the parsley and crab meat; blend well. Place this mixture in 6 well-greased individual shells or 5-ounce custard cups. Combine the fat and crumbs, and sprinkle over the top of each shell. Bake the crab in a moderate oven (350° F) for 20 to 25 minutes, or until it is brown. This recipe serves 6.

CRAB CAKES

2 slices bread
1 egg, slightly beaten
1 tablespoon mayonnaise
2 tablespoons parsley flakes
1 teaspoon celery salt
¼ teaspoon dry mustard
½ teaspoon savory
1 tablespoon Worcestershire
   sauce
1/8 teaspoon cayenne pepper
1 tablespoon baking powder
Dash of black pepper
1 pound crab meat
Shortening

Crumble the bread into small pieces and mix with the beaten egg. Add all the other ingredients and mix them thoroughly. Combine them with the crabmeat and shape into cakes. Fry the cakes in hot shortening or deep fat at 375° F for about four minutes or until they are golden brown.

CRAB HORS d'OEUVRE

1 (8 ounce) package cream
   cheese, softened
1 tablespoon milk
1 (8 ounce) can crabmeat
2 tablespoons chopped onion
½ teaspoon horseradish
Salt and pepper to taste
1 (2 ounce) package slivered
   almonds

Blend together the cream cheese, milk, crabmeat, onion, and horseradish. Add the salt and pepper. Place the mixture in a shallow baking dish. Sprinkle almonds over the top. Bake it at 350° F for 20 minutes or until it is lightly browned on top. Serve it hot on crackers or as a dip.

HOT CRAB AND
GREEN BEAN SALAD

¾ pound cooked crab meat or
    2 cans (6 ounce each) crab
    meat
1½ pounds green beans
¾ cup mayonnaise
2 tablespoons lemon juice
½ teaspoon dry mustard
1 small clove garlic, mashed
¼ cup finely chopped onion
¼ teaspoon salt
Few grains pepper
1/3 cup dry bread crumbs
¼ cup melted butter or margarine

Drain the crab meat. Remove any bits of shell or cartilage. Trim the green beans and cut them into 1" pieces. Cook the beans covered in boiling salted water for about 15 minutes, or until they are tender but still crisp. Drain them. You should have 4 cups of beans. Combine the mayonnaise, lemon juice, mustard, garlic, onion, salt, and pepper. Blend well. Mix this with the beans. Fold in the crab meat, taking care not to break it into shreds. Spoon the mixture into 8 greased scallop shells or small individual casseroles of about 6-ounce capacity. Top each dish with 2 teaspoons of bread crumbs. Saturate with melted butter. Bake the casserole in a moderately hot oven (400° F) until it is piping hot and the crumbs are browned. This will take about 15 minutes. This recipe makes 8 servings.

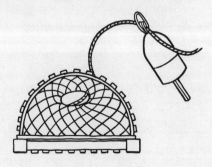

BAKED CRAB MEAT DELIGHT

1 can whole kernel corn
1 can peas, drained
1 can celery soup
1 small can mushrooms
  (don't drain)
1 pound frozen Alaskan
  crab meat, thawed
1 small can pimentos
Pepper to taste

Mix the above ingredients together and cover them with bread crumbs. Bake the mixture in a moderate oven (350°F) for 40 minutes. Canned or fresh crab meat may be substituted. You can also use other kinds of soup, such as mushroom or cream of chicken.

CRAB BISQUE

2 tablespoons butter
1½ teaspoons flour
1 can milk (or 1 cup cream)
3 cups milk
¼ cup chopped celery
1 can of crab meat
½ teaspoon salt
Pepper
Paprika

Melt the butter and stir in the flour; slowly stir in the milk. When the mixture thickens, add the canned milk, crab meat, salt, and pepper. Cook the sauce slowly in a double boiler, but do not boil the milk. Serve this with oyster crackers.

CRAB MEAT SALAD

1 pound crab meat
Lettuce
3 hard-boiled eggs
Green olives
Cocktail sauce

*Fill a small platter with crisp lettuce chunks. Spread
the crab meat over the lettuce and surround it with al-
ternating slices of eggs and olives. Dot the salad with
tangy fish sauce.*

CRABMEAT CHEESE BUNS

1 (6 ounce) package Velveeta cheese
¼ pound butter or margarine
1 can crabmeat
6 hamburger buns, cut in halves

*Cut the cheese and butter into cubes. Place them in a
covered saucepan and melt them over a low heat. Add
the crabmeat and mix. Spread this mixture on the buns.
Broil the buns about 4 inches from the heat until they
are golden brown.*

CRAB-CHEESE DIP

2 cans crab meat, drained
    (6½-7 ounces each, or thaw 2
    6½ ounce frozen packages)
1 box creamed cottage cheese
    (8 ounce)
2 tablespoons mayonnaise
1 tablespoon prepared mustard
1 tablespoon lemon juice
½ teaspoon salt

*Save half of the crab meat that is pink to use as a
garnish and mix the other half in your electric blender
with all the other ingredients. Whirl until blended.
Pile the dip on a serving dish and garnish it with the
remaining crab meat, parsley, and lemon slices.
(Contains about 27 calories.)*

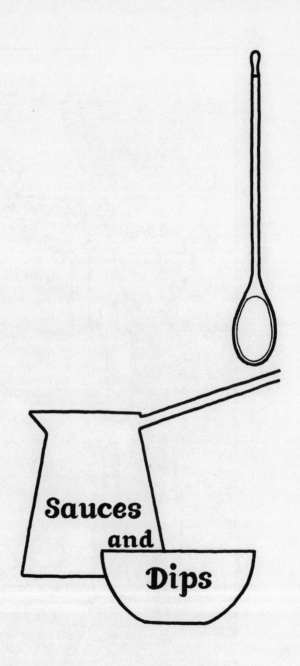

Sauces
and
Dips

TANGY FISH SAUCE

1¾ tablespoons horseradish
¾ cup tomato ketchup
3 tablespoons chili sauce
2 tablespoons lemon juice
Dash of salt

Mix the ingredients together, chill, and serve. This is a tasty cocktail sauce for those who wish to control their calorie count. It can be served with baked fish, shrimp, oysters, or with many kinds of fried fish. It is especially good with crab meat salad.

MUSTARD SAUCE

½ cup tomato soup
½ cup prepared mustard
½ cup vinegar
½ cup butter
3 beaten egg yolks

Cook the sauce until it is thick. If refrigerated, it will keep indefinitely. It is delicious with fish.

SEAFOOD SAUCE

½ cup chili sauce
1/3 cup ketchup
1/3 cup prepared horseradish
1½ teaspoons Worcestershire
    sauce
¼ teaspoon salt
2 tablespoons lemon juice
1/8 teaspoon pepper
¼ cup minced celery

Combine all the ingredients. Place the sauce in a jar and keep it covered and chilled. This recipe makes about 1½ cups.

LEMON BUTTER SAUCE

¼ cup melted butter or margarine
2 tablespoons lemon juice
1 teaspoon minced onion
Dash Tabasco

Combine the ingredients and mix them well.

TARTAR SAUCE

1 egg
1 teaspoon salt
1 teaspoon sugar
1 teaspoon mustard
Chopped sweet pickles
 (to taste)
6 teaspoons vinegar
6 teaspoons lemon juice
1½ cups olive oil
Pepper to taste

Add all the ingredients to the egg, except the oil; then beat them well. Add the oil by the tablespoon. Beat well after each addition.

TARTAR SAUCE

½ cup mayonnaise
2 tablespoons finely chopped
 sweet pickles
2 teaspoons finely grated
 onion
½ teaspoon Worcestershire
 sauce
1 tablespoon minced parsley

Mix the ingredients in a jar and, after stirring thoroughly, shake the jar until the sauce is well mixed. Cover the jar and refrigerate for the flavors to blend. (If you enjoy savory, add a pinch to your tartar sauce for a little different flavor.)

CHINESE SWEET AND
SOUR SAUCE

1 cup sugar
3 tablespoons cornstarch
1 cup white vinegar
1 cup cold water
3 tablespoons ketchup
1 teaspoon salt
1/8 teaspoon pepper
3 tablespoons cooking oil
2 large tomatoes, cut in wedges
Red food coloring (optional)

Combine the sugar and cornstarch. To the mixture, add the vinegar and water, then stir until they are dissolved. Add the ketchup, seasonings, cooking oil, and tomatoes. Bring the sauce to a boil. Cook, stirring constantly, until the sauce is clear and thickened. Stir in the food coloring, drop by drop, until the desired color intensity is obtained. This recipe makes 2½ cups.

CHILI SHRIMP DIP

1 can (10 ounce) frozen condensed
  cream of shrimp soup
1 package (8 ounce) cream cheese,
  softened
2 tablespoons chopped parsley
1 tablespoon finely chopped green
  pepper
1 teaspoon finely chopped pimento
1 teaspoon chili powder

Thaw the soup by placing the unopened can in a pan of hot water for about 30 minutes. Combine the soup with the cheese and beat it until it is smooth with a rotary beater or electric mixer (overbeating will make the dip thin). Add the remaining ingredients and chill. Serve the dip with crackers or chips. This recipe makes about 2 cups.

TIPSY HERRING APPETIZER

1 jar (12 ounces) herring in wine
  sauce
1 can (10½ ounces) tomato aspic
6 lettuce leaves
Sour cream sauce

Drain the herring, reserving the sauce. Cut the herring into 1" pieces. Chill the aspic. Remove the aspic from the can and cut it into 6 crosswise slices. Place a slice of aspic on each lettuce leaf. Arrange the herring on the aspic. Top each serving with approximately 1 tablespoon of sour cream sauce. This recipe serves 6.

SOUR CREAM SAUCE

1/3 cup sour cream
1-1/3 tablespoons wine sauce
1 teaspoon lemon juice
¼ teaspoon salt
¼ teaspoon dill weed

Combine all the ingredients and mix them thoroughly. Chill the sauce for at least 1 hour to blend the flavors. This recipe makes approximately ½ cup of sauce.

SHRIMP DIP

1/3 cup cream
1 (8 ounce) package cream
  cheese
2 teaspoons lemon juice
¼ teaspoon onion juice
Dash Worcestershire sauce
¾ cup cooked or canned
  shrimp, chopped

Gradually add the cream to the cream cheese, mixing them until they are well blended. Then add the rest of the ingredients. This dip is delicious with crackers or chips.

MEXICAN BARBECUE SAUCE

1 cup olive oil
1 cup tomato juice
½ cup vinegar
3 tablespoons finely minced
   shallots (you can substitute
   onion)
1 tablespoon chili powder
3 tablespoons green pepper
1 teaspoon salt
1 teaspoon oregano
4 garlic cloves, crushed

This barbecue sauce is excellent for basting grilled fish and meats. Combine all the ingredients and simmer gently for 10 minutes. Strain the sauce and use it for basting fish or meats.

HOLLANDAISE SAUCE

¼ cup butter
1 tablespoon flour
2 egg yolks, beaten
¾ cup boiling water
Juice of 1 lemon
Salt
Paprika
Red pepper

Mix the butter and flour until smooth. Put the mixture in a double boiler. Add the egg yolks. Add boiling water and keep stirring the sauce until it is sufficiently thick. When ready to serve the sauce, add the juice of a lemon; use a rotary beater to mix it in. Add salt and paprika.

Spiced cranberries, cranberry mold, cranberry sauce, chili sauce, fried apple rings, glazed pineapple, beet relish, cinnamon apples, or applesauce are all delicious relishes suitable to be served with the many varieties of fish.

INDEX